Comprehensive English for Hoteliers

Mando Park

Hong Ick Publishing Co.

머 리 말

세계화에 부응하여 관광산업분야에서도 영어 구사력의 중요성은 무엇보다도 중요하다 하겠다. 짧은 시간에 관광산업의 모든 분야의 실무를 영어로 완벽하게 구사하는 것은 힘든 실정이므로 단일 분야로 볼 때 큰 분야에 속하는 호텔 분야에서 기본적이며 반드시 알아야 할 표현력을 습득하는 것이 필요하리라 본다.

호텔 분야에서만 쓰이는 영어 구사력이란 실제로 있을 수는 없겠지만 편의상 호텔 분야에서 많이 사용되는 영어 표현들을 정리하여 현장에서 실무능력을 향상시키는데 그 목적이 있다.

학습자들의 학습 동기를 부여하기 위해서 될 수 있는 대로 이해하기 쉽고 가장 쉬운 표현과 간략한 대화 구성으로 이루어지게 하였다. 짧은 대화와 평이한 내용으로 실무능력을 향상시키는데 초점을 두었다.

호텔 분야의 기본적이며 필수적인 쉬운 표현들로 구성된 단원으로 세분화하였다. 관광산업 분야에 관한 기초 독해와 호텔 분야에서 널리 사용되는 용어 풀이도 포함시켰다.

또한 국외여행가이드 및 비서실무 분야에서 기본적이고, 필수적인 표현력을 습득하는 것이 중요하며 호텔산업 뿐만 아니라 폭넓은 관광산업 분야에서도 활용가능한 기본적이며 필수적인 표현들로 구성되어있다.

아무튼 실무영어 학습에서 기본적인 영어 회화 표현과 더불어 관광산업분야의 특성을 이해하고서 업무수행능력을 배양하는 것이 중요하리라 생각되며 호텔리어를 꿈꾸는 학생들에게 하나의 작은 길잡이가 되기를 바라며 또한 관광산업분야 중에서도 호텔 분야에 관심이 있는 학습자들에게 도움이 되었으면 한다. 출판에 도움을 주신 홍익출판사 김창석 사장님과 그 직원들께 감사를 드린다.

2012. 8

CONTENTS

Part Ⅰ

Unit 1
Unit 2
Unit 3
Unit 4
Unit 5
Unit 6
Unit 7
Unit 8
Unit 9
Unit 10
Unit 11

❖ Unit 1 Reservation ❖

예약은 전화, 서신, 전신, 혹은 프론트 데스크에서 직접 할 수 있다. 작은 호텔에서는 프론트 데스크에서 예약이 이루어지며 큰 호텔에서는 독립적인 예약 부서가 있다.

예약을 취급함에 있어서 직원은 예약자의 이름, 객실의 형태와 수, 체류기간, 도착시간, 그리고 항공기와 번호 등을 기록해야 한다.

Section I

Dialogue 1

R : Reservation Clerk
G : Guest

R : Good morning, Hotel Grand, Reservation Desk.
May I help you?

G : Yes. I'd like to reserve a room.

R : What kind of room would you like, sir?

G : Oh, I'd like to reserve a single room for tomorrow night.

R : I'm so sorry, but we have no single rooms available for tomorrow night.

G : Could you give me the name of another hotel?

R : Why don't you try Park Hotel, ma'am?

G : Park Hotel. Thank you so much.

R : It's my pleasure. Thank you for calling.

Dialogue 2

R : Reservation Clerk

G : Guest

R : Good morning, Hotel Susong, Reservation Desk.

May I help you?

G : Yes. I'd like to reserve a room.

R : What kind of room would you like, sir?

G : A suite for my family.

R : How long are you going to stay here, sir?

G : It depends.

But we will be staying for about a week.

Dialogue 3

R : Reservation clerk

G : Guest

R : Korean Air, Miss Kim speaking.

May I help you?

G : Yes. I'd like to reserve a seat to New York.

R : When would you like to make it for, sir?

G : The 4 : 00 p.m flight on Tuesday.

R : Would you like economy class or first class, sir?

G : Economy class, please.

R : Would you like a round trip ticket?

G : Yes.

I should be back in Seoul on Wednesday.

R : May I have your name and phone number, please?

G : John Miller 744-9316

R : Thank you for calling.

Dialogue 4

R : Reservation clerk

T : Tourist

R : Good afternoon, May I help you, sir?

T : I'd like to make a reservation for dinner.

R : How many members in your group, sir?

T : There are eight people.

R : What time would you like to have your dinner, sir?

T : About 8 : 00 p.m.

R : May I have your name and phone number, please?

T : My name is John Peter at 744-9316.

R : Thank you, sir.

Your reservation has been made.

Dialogue 5

I : Immigration Officer

P : Passenger

I : May I have your passport and arrival card?

P : Here you are.

I : Where are you from?

P : I'm from Seoul.

I : Is this your first visit to Japan?

P : Yes. It is.

I : What's the purpose of your visit?

P : For an International Convention.

I : How long are you staying in Tokyo?

P : It depends.

But for about a week.

I : Thank you.

Section Ⅱ

Dialogue 1

C : Clerk

G : Guest

C : What can I do for you, sir?

G : Yes, I'd like to get a room.

C : Do you have a reservation, sir?

G : Yes. I do.

C : What type of room did you reserve, sir?

G : Single room, please.

C : I'm sorry, sir. Our single rooms are all filled up.

But we have some double rooms.

You don't have to pay for it at a double room rate.

G : You mean I can use a double room at a single room rate?

C : That's right.

G : Thank you.

Dialogue 2

C : Room Clerk
G : Guest

C : Good evening, may I help you, sir?

G : Yes, please.
I have a reservation.

C : May I have your name, sir?

G : John Smith.

C : Yes, your reservation has been made.
Your room is a single on the tenth floor.
Would you fill out this card, sir?

G : Here you are.
Is this okay?

C : Perfect, sir.
May I have your passport for a moment, please?

G : Here it is.

C : Thank you, sir.

Dialogue 3

C : Clerk
G : Guest

C : Good evening, sir.
May I help you?
G : My name is John Pak.
I'd like a single room for three nights.
C : Yes.
We have your reservation through Hotel Susong.
Would you complete this card, please?
G : Here it is.
C : May I have your passport for a moment, sir?
G : Here's my passport.
C : Thank you, sir.
Here's your key.
Our bellman will show you to your room, No. 1204.
G : Thank you.

Dialogue 4

C : Clerk
G : Guest

C : What can I do for you, sir?

G : I made a reservation for a double room
What's the room rate for a double room?

C : US $ 100 plus tax and service charge, sir.

G : Then, how much will it come to?

C : Ten percent national tax and another ten percent service charge will be added to that, sir.
The total will be US $ 121.

G : I see.

C : Would you complete this registration card, please?

G : Sure.
Here it is.

C : Thank you, sir.
Your room is 1202.
Here's your room key.
Our bellman will take care of your baggage, sir.

Dialogue 5

C : Clerk

G : Guest

C : Good afternoon, Reservation. How can I help you?

G : I'd like to book a room, please.

C : When do you plan to check in, sir?

G : October 13th

C : Let me first check the room availability, sir.

How long will you be staying in our hotel, sir?

G : 3 nights.

C : So, you are going to check out on Friday October 16th.

Is that correct, sir?

G : That's correct.

C : What type of room would you like, sir?

G : A single room with a city view if possible.

C : Yes, we have a single room available on the 16th floor.

Section III

Dialogue 1

C : Clerk

G : Guest

C : Good afternoon Reservation. Can I help you?

G : Yes. Do you have any rooms available tonight?

C : Yes, ma'am. What type of room would you like?

G : A double room on a non-smoking floor if you have one.

C : Just a moment, please. I'll check it right away, ma'am.

G : That's okay. I'll take it. By the way, what's the room rate?

C : 200.000 won per night, ma'am.

How long do you plan to stay?

G : Oh, just for tonight, please.

C : May I have your name and number?

G : Mr. Park and my phone number is 744－9316

Dialogue 2

C : Clerk
G : Guest

C : Good afternoon, may I help you?

G : Yes, please. I'd like to reserve a room.

C : What kind of room would you like, ma'am?

G : A double room with a nice view if possible.

C : When would you like to stay here, ma'am?

G : Form Marth 3rd to 11th.

C : Just moment, please. We have a very nice room with a good view of Kumho-River available.

G : That's great. But what's the room rate?

C : US$ 100.00 a night.

Dialogue 3

C : Clerk

G : Guest

C : Good afternoon. Reservations. May I help you?

G : I'd like to book a room.

C : Thank you. Which date would that be, sir?

G : February 12th.

C : How many days will you stay, sir?

G : There days.

C : What kind of room would you like, sir?

G : Well I'm traveling with my wife. So I need a double room in the non-smoking floor, please.

Dialogue 4

C : Clerk

G : Guest

C : When is your arrival time at the Daegu Airport. Mr. Park?

G : 8 : 10 a.m local time.

C : Thanks. Do you need a rental car service, sir?

G : No, thanks. By the way, is there any shuttle service between the airport and your hotel?

C : Centainly, sir. Please take airport limousine bus No.3 which will bring you to our hotel directly.

G : That's great. Thanks.

Dialogue 5

C : Clerk

G : Guest

G : Have you got any room for tonight?

C : Yes, sir. Single room is it?

G : Yes. If possible with a river a view, please.

C : Yes. And for how long, sir?

G : Just one night.

C : Fine. Our best rate I can offer you for tonight is 140.000 won excluding V.A.T and service charge. Is that fine with you?

G : Yes. That'll be fine.

Key Expressions

II

1. What's type of single would you like?
2. What's kind of room would you like?
3. Can you spell your last name sir?
4. Your room has been reserved from October 13th to 15th
5. We'll be expecting you next week.
6. Do you have any rooms available tonight?
7. Have you got any room for tonight?
8. Is that all light with you, ma'am?
9. What time will you be arriving?
10. What's the room rate?
11. How much would that be in US dollar?
12. It depends on the exchange rate on the day you check in, sir.
13. What would the charge be?
14. We look forward to seeing you.
15. Please give me the reservation desk.

Basic Vocabulary

reservation
reservation chart[1)]
reservation diary[2)]
reservation form[3)]
reservation rack[4)]
density chart[5)]
single room[6)]
double room[7)]
twin room[8)]
triple room[9)]
penthouse[10)]
suite[11)]
lounge
parlor
room charge
room rate
service charge
special charge
vacant room
vacancy
living room
executive floor[12)]
manager
full house
brochure
pamphlet
connecting room
adjoining room

---

1) 예약도표
2) 예약일지
3) 예약양식
4) 예약꽂이
5) 예약 분포도
6) 1인용 침대가 있는 객실
7) 2인용 침대가 있는 객실
8) 1인용 침대가 2개 있는 객실
9) 3인이 투숙할 수 있는 객실
10) 옥상에 있는 suite
11) 1실 이상의 침실, 거실, 주방 등이 갖춰진 대형객실
12) 비즈니스 업무 고객들을 위한 객실들이 있는 특별층

❖ Unit 2 Reception ❖

고객이 호텔데스크에 도착하면, 직원은 친절하고 미소를 띄면서 인사를 해야 한다. 직원은 고객에게 온갖 주위를 기울여서 조심스럽게 그리고 예의 바르게 귀담아 들어야 한다.

프론트 데스크의 모든 직원은 고객을 투숙시키는 단계적인 절차를 숙지하고 있어야 한다. 호텔마다 나름내로의 투숙절차가 있겠지만 거의 비슷하다.

Section I

Dialogue 1

C : Clerk

G : Guest

C : Good afternoon, may I help you sir?

G : Yes, please. I reserved a single room three weeks ago and I'm Mr. Kim.

C : Just moment, please. Mr. Kim. Let me check on it for you.

(*After checking it in the computer)*

A single room for three nights. Is that correct. Mr. Kim?

G : That's right.

C : Please fill out this registration card.

G : Yes. Here you are.

Dialogue 2

C : Clerk
G : Guest

C : Good morning sir? May I help you?

G : Yes. My name is John Smith. I have a reservation.

C : One moment, please. Yes. we have a reservation, a double room with a city view for 3 nights, Mr. Smith.

G : That's it.

C : Would you please fill out this registration card?
Your room number is 1834.

G : Sure. By the way, what's the room rate?

C : US$150.00 a night.

Dialogue 3

C : Clerk

G : Guest

C : Good afternoon. May I help you?

G : Yes. I'm John Smith. Do you have a reservation for us?

C : Mr. John Smith···Just a minute, sir. I'll check on it for you.

Yes, I have your reservation.

G : That's correct.

C : Will you please complete this registration card, Mr. Smith?

What are the rates?

C : 150,000 Won for the double per night.

G : Okay. I'll take it.

Dialogue 4

C : Clerk
G : Guest

C : Good afternoon. May I help you?

G : Yes, I'd like to check in, please.

C : Do you have a reservation with us?

G : Yes, I do.

C : May I have your name, please.

G : Smith John Smith.

C : Could you fill out the from, please, Mr. Smith?

G : Alright.

C : Thank you very much.

Dialogue 5

C : Clerk
G : Guest

C : Good evening. May I help you, sir?

G : Yes, please. I have a reservation here.

C : May I have your name, please.

G : Jones Smith.

C : Oh, yes. We have your reservation. A double room with a city view, room 1234, Mr. Smith.

G : That's fine.

C : Would you please complete this card?

G : Sure. Here you are.

Section Ⅱ

Dialogue 1

C : Clerk

G : Guest

C : Good evening, sir. Welcome to Grand Hotel.

May I help you?

G : Yes, please. I need a room for tonight.

C : Do you have a reservation, sir?

G : No, I don't.

C : Just a moment, sir. Let me check the room availability for tonight. The only room we have left is a Junior Suite.

G : What's the room rate?

C : It's 250,000 won

Dialogue 2

C : Clerk
G : Guest

C : Good evening. sir. May I help you?

G : Good evening. Is there any room available for tonight?

C : Yes, there is.

G : What's the rate for a double?

C : US$160.00 a right.

How long are you planning to stay?

G : Just one night.

C : Alright. Please fill out this registration card.

C : Okay. Here's the card.

C : Thanks. Here's your key.

Dialogue 3

R : Receptionist

G : Guest

R : Good morning. Can I help you?

G : Good morning. My name is Baker. James R. Baker.
I have booked a room by phone.

R : What's your reservation number, Mr Baker?

G : Here you are.

R : Thank you. Just a moment. please. I'll check it... That's all right, Mr. Baker. One single room has been reserved up to March 12th. Will you stay until then?

G : Yes, I think so.

Dialogue 4

C : Clerk
G : Guest

G : Can you help me with this form, please?
My English isn't very good.

C : Yes, of course, sir …let's see … yes… The frist thing is your family name … What's your family name, please?

G : Ah, my family name. Yes, it's Smith.

C : Smith. How do you spell that?

G : S−M−I−T−H

C : Thank you and your first name?

G : It's, er…John.

Dialogue 5

C : Clerk

G : Guest

G : Hello.

I'd like to reserve a room for two adults and a child for Sunday the 4th of October.

C : Sunday the 4th of October, two adults and a child, and how long would you be staying?

G : For two nights.

C : We could give you a twin room and put an extra bed in it. Would that be suitable?

G : What would the charge be?

C : How old is the child?

G : He's seven.

C : Well, there would be no charge for the child.

Key Expressions

I

1. Do you have a reservation, sir?
2. I have a reservation under the name of Smith.
3. What's your reservation number?
4. Let me check on it for you.
5. Would you please fill in this registration card?
6. Could you fill this form out?
7. Will you please complete this registration card?
8. Would you fill this form out?
9. Can I see your ID please ?
10. Are those rooms next to each other?
11. The Bellman will show you to your room.
12. That's rather expensive.
13. We're all booked up.
14. I'm sorry, we're fully booked up the moment.
15. Could you check with other hotel for me?

Key Expressions

II

1. I'd like to book a room, please.
2. I'd like to reserve a room.
3. For when would you like the room?
4. How long will you be staying in our hotel, sir?
5. How many days will you stay?
6. How many nights are you planing to stay?
7. How long do you plan to stay ?
8. Until when are you intending to stay?
9. When do you plan to check in, sir?
10. Which date would that be sir?
11. When would you like to stay here, ma'am?
12. Have you any idea when you'd be arriving sir?
13. Would like a room in the front or back of the hotel?
14. I'd prefer a room facing south, on the second floor.
15. Let me frist check the room availability, ma'am.

Key Expressions

Ⅲ

1. The currently available room rates for that period are US$170.00 for a single.
2. The room rate would be US$140 per night and 10% V.A.T and 10% service charge will be added to it.
3. The government tax and service charge will be added to this rate.
4. Is there any way to give me a better rate than that?
5. Can we have a discount for it?
6. That's the best rates I can offer you now, sir.
7. That's the best rate available for now.
8. To make a reservation I need your name and phone number, please?
9. We'll hold the room for you.
10. Have you already booked your flight, sir?
11. I am supposed to be picked up by my business partner at the airport.
12. Please reconfirm your reservation the latest 7 days prior to your reservation date.
13. Thank you for choosing the Grand hotel.
14. We have a very nice room with a good view of Kumho-River available.
15. Could you hold the line, please?

Basic Vocabulary

availability[1]
period
peak
spell
choose
forward
regards
terrace
luxury
client
bouquet
room rate
executive
offer
complimentary[2]
shuttle
conference
obviously
attractive
ideal
conccrned

1) 이용도, 이용될 수 있는 것
2) 무료의

❖ Unit 3 Check-In Service ❖

투숙 절차에 있어서 우선 손님에게 예의 바르게 인사를 하고 난 후 예약을 했는지를 물어본다. 예약 없이 직접 온 손님이라면 빈방이 있는지를 확인하고 손님을 만족시킬 수 있는 방을 제시한다. 손님이 등록카드에 서명과 주소를 적고 나서 성명, 객실번호, 요금 등과 같은 필요한 정보들을 기입한다. 그런 후에 벨맨이 와서 도움을 주게 된다.

Section Ⅰ

Dialogue 1

C : Clerk
G : Guest

C : Good evening, can I help you?

G : Yes, I'd like a room for three nights.

C : Do you have a reservation?

G : Yes, the name's Johnson. I telephoned you on March 3rd.

C : Ah yes, Mr. Johnson. Could you fill in this registration card, please?

G : Is it necessary to fill in the passport information?

C : Yes, if you would, please. Here's your Key. It's room 3050 on the third floor. And here's your Key card for use in the hotel's bars and restaurants. I'll ask the bellman to help you with your baggage.

Dialogue 2

C : Clerk
G : Guest

C : Good evening, may I help you, sir?

G : Yes, please.
I have a reservation.

C : May I have your name, sir?

G : John Smith.

C : Yes, your reservation has been made.
Your room is a single on the tenth floor.
Would you fill out this card, sir?

G : Here you are.
Is this okay?

C : Perfect, sir.
May I have your passport for a moment, please?

G : Here it is.

C : Thank you, sir.
Here's your room Key, room 104.
I'll have a bellman take your baggage up to your room.

Dialogue 3

C : Clerk
G : Guest

C : Good afternoon, sir. May I have your name?

G : Kim is my name.

C : How do you spell your name, sir?

G : K-I-M. I have a reservation for three nights.

C : One moment, sir··· Yes, a single room with a bath, isn't it?

G : Yes, that's right.

C : We have a room ready for you on the third floor··· room 352.

G : I hope it's a quiet room.

C : I can assure you the room is very quiet.

G : Fine. And how much is it?

C : It's 85,000 won a night, sir.

Dialogue 4

C : Clerk
G : Guest

C : Good evening, sir, May I help you?

G : My name is John Smith. I have a reservation.

C : Just a moment, sir. I'll check the list··· Mr. Smith··· Yes, we have your reservation. That was a double room, right?

G : Right.

C : Would you fill out this registration form, please?

G : All right. Here you go.

C : Thank you very much. Here is your key. Your room number is 1205. The bellman will show you to your room. Have a pleasant stay, sir!

Dialogue 5

C : Clerk

G : Guest

G : Good afternoon. I've made a reservation.

C : What was the name, sir?

G : McDonald, Jack McDonald.

C : Mr. McDonald, Yes. One moment. Ah, here we are. That's a single room for two nights?

G : That's right.

C : That's fine, Mr. McDonald. I've put you in room 820. It's on the eighth floor.

G : OK.

C : If you'd just like to fill in this registration card.

G : All right.

C : And then the bellman will take you up to your room.

G : Thank you.

Section Ⅱ

Dialogue 1

C : Clerk

B : Mr. Brown

B : My mame is Brown. I have a reservation here for two nights.

C : Just a moment, sir··· Yes, Mr. Brown. We have a single room reserved for you. Would you please fill in this registration card?

B : All right.

C : Please be sure to write your passport number on the card.

B : Here it is.

C : Thank you, sir. Here's the key to your room.

Dialogue 2

C : Clerk

G : Guest

C : Good afternoon. Reservation.

How may I help you?

G : Hello. I'd like to reserve a room for two adults and a child for Tuesday, the fourth of September.

C : Tuesday, the fourth of September…two adult and a child … and how long would you be staying?

G : For two nights.

Dialogue 3

C : Clerk
G : Guest

G : Good afternoon! I'm the tour guide of the Lucky Tour Agency.

C : Good afternoon. Welcome to our hotel. I'd like to reconfirm the schedule for the period of your stay. Is there any change in the number of your group?

G : Well, I'm afraid we're had some last minute changes.

Dialogue 4

C : Clerk

G : Guest

C : Good morning, sir. May I help you?

G : Yes. I'd like to pay my bill.

C : Yes, sir. What's your room number and name?

G : Room 1252 and my name is Richard Biller.

C : Are you leaving today, Mr. Biller?

G : Yes, I am. How much is the total?

C : It's 900,000 Won.

Dialogue 5

C : Clerk
G : Guest

C : Can I have your name and phone number, please?

G : Certainly. It's John Smith and my number is 212-356-9823.

C : How do you spell your last name sir?

G : S-M-I-T-H

C : Thank you. Mr, Smith. May I have your airline and flight number, please?

Key Expressions

I

1. Would you please register?
2. Would you fill in this registration card?
3. How many rooms do you need?
4. How many people are there in your party?
5. What's your family name?
6. What's your nationality?
7. May I see your passport, please?
8. Where was the passport issued?
9. Where are you going after this?
10. How do you spell your name, sir?
11. Shall I find another hotel for you?
12. When did you make reservation?
13. Is there a special rate by the week?
14. Can I extend my stay for anther night?
15. I hope you will enjoy your stay in our hotel.

Key Expressions

II

1. We can give you these rooms on the same floor but not adjoining.
2. Is breakfast included in it?
3. Breakfast is included in the rate only for the room on the Executive floor.
4. The Bellman will be here any minute to bring your luggage up to your room.
5. I will have someone take your baggage up to your room right away.
6. Other hotels in this area are sold out as well.
7. Do you know of any other hotels around here I could check?
8. It seems like I have no other choice but take it.
9. I would appreciate it if you could give me a discount on it.
10. Please give me the reservation desk.
11. The rate will be 150 dollars a night including breakfast.
12. What would the charge be?
13. I'd like reserve a room for two adults and a child.
14. We look forward to seeing you.
15. Will you make out separate bills for us?

Basic Vocabulary

registration

registration clerk

registration card[1)]

front desk

family name

address

nationality

signature

passport

place of issue

plaue of birth

no show[2)]

discount

European plan[3)]

Continental plan[4)]

American plan[5)]

Modified American plan[6)]

bedroom card[7)]

passport information

---

1) 고객등록카드
2) 예약을 해 놓고 손님이 나타나지 않는 경우
3) 식대를 포함하지 않은 객실요금
4) 객실과 조반을 포함하는 요금
5) 객실과 모든 식대를 포함하는 요금. full board 혹은 en pension
7) 고객의 투숙을 확인해 주는 카드

❖ Unit 4 Bellman and Doorman ❖

손님에게 호텔의 첫 인상을 주는 사람이 도어맨과 벨맨이다. 그들은 호텔의 입구에 위치해 있으며 모든 손님들을 맞이한다. 손님에게 택시도 불러주고 배웅도 한다. 도어맨은 또한 고객이 타고 온 차량을 위해 호텔 주차지역도 관리한다. 근무시간에는 유니폼을 착용하고 있으며 모든 고개들에게 직접 도움을 주고 있다. 벨맨은 손님들을 객실로 안내하며 객실 등의 사용법을 설명해 준다. 손님들의 수하물도 운반해 주며 퇴숙할시에도 손님의 짐을 로비까지 가져다준다.

Section Ⅰ

Dialogue 1

C : Clerk
B : Bellman

B : This way, please. I'll show you to your room. The elevator is over there.

G : Thank you.

B : Here, we're on the 15th floor. Room 1503 is on your left side. This is your room. Please get in.

G : It's a very nice room.

B : I'm glad that you like it, sir. Is there anything else I can do for you, sir?

G : No, I don't think so.

B : Well, if you need any help, please feel free to call bell desk.

G : I'll do that. Thank you very much.

Dialogue 2

B : Bellman
G : Guest

B : Good morning, sir.
Are these all yours, sir?

G : Yes, but two more pieces of baggage will come from the airport.

B : This way, please.
This is your room 607.

G : This room looks comfortable.

B : Thank you, sir.
All the stationary is in the desk drawer, sir.
Anything else I can help you with, sir?

G : That will be all.

B : Enjoy your stay.

Dialogue 3

B : Bellman
G : Guest

B : Here is the light switch for the bathroom.

G : How do I call room service?

B : Please dial 3, ma'am. Room service operates 24 hours a day, so feel free to use it any time you want.

G : Can I have some paper and envelopes? I need to write some letters.

B : All stationery is in the desk drawer, ma'am. Is there anything else I can do for you?

G : Yes, how late does the beauty shop stay open?

B : Until 9 p.m, ma'am.

G : Thank you very much.

Dialogue 4

C : Clerk
G : Guest

G : I want to do some sightseeing around this country. Could I get some tour information?

C : How long are you going to stay here, sir?

G : We are going to stay three more days.

C : In that case, you may want to go to the Everland in Yong-In. We have shuttle bus leaving at 10 tomorrow morning.

G : Yes, I'm very much interested in that. Put us on the list, please.

C : How large is your party?

G : My wife, two kids, and myself.

C : Your name, please?

G : Jerry Scott from room 1815.

Dialogue 5

B : Bellman
G : Guest

B : Are these all your bags, sir?

G : Yes, these are all ; two bags and a golf bag.

B : Any other baggage coming, sir?

G : Yes, I've got two more pieces coming.

B : Oh, I see. Now, this way, please…… Here we are. After you, sir.

G : This room looks nice.

B : Thank you, sir. It commands a fine view of the lake… The built-in closet is here and the bathroom over there.

G : I want to send a cable. Will you get me a cable form?

B : All stationery is in this desk drawer. There arc also a room service menu and a brochure listing all the services of the hotel.

G : Thank you. Here you are.

B : I'm sorry, but no tipping is our pride.

Section Ⅱ

Dialogue 1

B : Bellman
G : Guest

B : Are these all your bags, Mr. Tom?

G : Yes, but I'll carry this one.

B : Let me show you to your room, sir.
This way to the elevator, please.

G : Alight.

B : Where shall I put your bags?

G : Just here, thank.

B : Is there anything else I can do?

G : No, thanks.

B : Enjoy your stay, Mr. Tom.

Dialogue 2

B : Bellman

G : Guest

B : Concierge Desk. May I help you?

G : I will be checking out pretty soon.

Could you pick up my luggage, please?

B : Centainly, sir. What's your room number, sir?

G : Room 1267.

B : I will send a Bellman to your room right away, sir.

G : Thank you.

Dialogue 3

B : Bellman
G : Guest

B : Good afternoon. Concierge Desk. How may I help you?

G : This is room 1305 and I have a very heavy luggage in my room. Can someone help me with it?

B : No problem, sir. I'll send a porter up to your room to carry it down for immediately, sir.

G : That would be very nice. Thanks a lot.

B : With pleasure, sir.

Dialogue 4

B : Bellman

G : Guest

G : Is there a sightseeing bus tour?

B : Yes, would you like one-day tour or a half-day tour?

G : One day.

B : How about going for a day trip to Folk Village?

G : That sounds good.

Can I make a reservation for tomorrow?

B : Centainly, for how many persons?

G : Two, please. My name is Tom.

B : All right. Please be at the Front Desk at 9 a.m. tomorrow.

Dialogue 5

B : Bellman

G : Guest

G : We'd like to go to the Korean Classical Dances at the King Sejong Cultural Center tomorrow evening.
Can you get us some tickets?

B : Sure. How many tickets do you need, sir?

G : Six, please.

B : Just a moment, please.

Key Expressions

I

1. May I help you with your baggage?
2. How many bags do you have in all?
3. Thank you. But no tipping is our pride.
4. Mind your hands in the revolving door.
5. There are no regular taxis here now.
6. I will show you to your room.
7. Any other baggage coming, sir?
8. Where shall I put your baggage, sir?
9. The stationery and hotel brochures are here.
10. You'll be charged for what you drink.
11. Please make use of it anytime.
12. Would you like me to reserve a table for you?
13. How do I call the room service?
14. Does the room door lock itself?
15. If you require other services, just contact No. 2 bell desk.

Key Expressions

II

1. It could happen that way.
2. I'll come along with him.
3. I'm afraid we need to make a little change.
4. How do you want to change it?
5. How long will it take to bring up all the bags to each room?
6. Can't you do something about the service in this hotel?
7. I'll deal with this myself.
8. What's the trouble exactly?
9. There's obviously been a misunderstanding between us.
10. Who's is overall charge of the hotel?
11. The Porter will be pleased to help you to arrange kennel facilities.
12. I'm sure you would find it satisfactory.
13. There's nothing further I can tell you.
14. You're not to be admitted to the hotel.
15. I demand an explanation.

Key Expressions

III

1. I'll send a porter up to your room to carry it down for you immediately.
2. I've knocked over a plate of food in my room.
3. Could someone possibly come and help clear up the mess?
4. They've been stolen outside my room.
5. Can you tell me what they look like?
6. Just let me get clear what happened.
7. Has the luggage gone up already?
8. All the rooms got their baggage okay.
9. Where did that thing go?
10. Thanks for the waiting, sir.
11. When is your arrival time at the Daegu airport?
12. Is there any shuttle service between the airport and your hotel?
13. Would that be suitable?
14. We look forward to seeing you.
15. We'll then expect you.

Basic Vocabulary

baggage
baggage rack
luggage
suitcase
briefcase
bellman[1)]
bellhop[2)]
doorman
porter
concierge[3)]
courier[4)]
cubbyhole[5)]
stationery
clothes hanger
built-in closet[6)]
revolving door
complimentary[7)]
refrigerator
automatic
taxi stand
brochure
air conditioning
heating
tour leader[8)]
rooming list[9)]
desk drawer

---

1) 등록을 마친 고객을 객실로 안내해 주며 고객 수하물의 운반 및 보관을 도와준다.
2) 짐을 나르거나 심부름을 하는 사람
3) 접객담당
4) 심부름꾼
5) 작은 칸막이 함
6) 객실내의 붙박이장
7) 무료의(free of charge(F.O.C))
8) 투숙하는 단체고객의 인솔자(escort, conductor)
9) 단체 투숙객의 사전 등록 및 객실 배정을 위한 투숙객의 명단

❖ Unit 5 Telephone Operator ❖

호텔의 전화 교환 수는 중요한 서비스 중의 하나를 담당하고 있다.
목소리를 통하여 호텔을 대표한다고 볼 수 있다. 그러므로 호텔 교환수는 예의 바르고 도움이 되게 정확하고 신속하게 서비스를 제공해야 한다.

Section I

Dialogue 1

O : Operator
G : Guest

G : Operator? I'd like to make an overseas call to New York.

O : May I have your name and room number, please?

G : Yes. Room 1342 and this is John.

O : Thank you, sir. Is it a person-to-person call, sir?

G : Yes. The party I want to call is Mr. Murphy.
The number is 536-7843.

O : Mr. Murphy, New York 536-7843?

G : That's right.

O : Hold the line, please. It will be connected right away.

Dialogue 2

O : Operator
G : Guest

O : Operator. May I help you?

G : Yes. How can I make a local call?

O : If you want to make a local call, simply dial "0" and then the number you wish to call. In case you need the local operator's assistance, dial "0" first, and then "114" that will get you in touch with the local operator, sir.
Is there anything else that I can do for you?

G : No, that's all, Thanks a lot.

Dialogue 3

O : Operator
G : Guest

O : Good morning. Operator. May I help you?

G : Yes. I'd like to make a long distance call to Germany.

O : May I have your name and room number, please?

G : Richard in room 1435.

O : Thank you. What number do you wish to call?

G : The area code is 212 and the number is 342-5672

O : Hold the line, please. I'll connect you immediately.

G : Thank you.

Dialogue 4

O : Operator
G : Guest

G : Operator, I want to place a long distance call to Los Angeles, please. Are there special night rates from here?

O : Yes, the night rates are from seven in the evening until four-thirty in the morning.

G : What time is it in Los Angeles now?

O : There is a time difference of seven hours. It is twenty-five past nine there now.

G : Fine, I'd like to put a call in now.

O : Just a minute. I'll connect you with the long distance.

Dialogue 5

O : Operator
G : Guest

G : Could you make the call for me? I speak only English.

O : All long distance operators speak English, sir.

G : But I don't want the call to put on my bill. I want to charge it on my credit card.

O : What is the number of your card?

G : It's 715856, American Society Card.

O : Thank you, sir. I'll get the long distance and report the charges to you later.

Section II

Dialogue 1

O : Operator
G : Guest

O : Operator, may I help you sir?

G : Yes. Is your Room Service available now?

O : Of course, sir.
Our Room service is open for twenty four hours.
Just dial 5 and order thc food you'd like to have, using the menu on the table.

G : How long will it take to be ready?
I'm very hungry.

O : It depends, sir.
But it doesn't take too long.

G : Thank you.

O : Enjoy your dinner.

Dialogue 2

C : Clerk
G : Guest

C : Good afternoon, sir. Can I help you?

G : Yes. I phoned on Friday to book a room.

C : What name is your reservation under?

G : Brown.

C : Ah yes, Mr. Brown, a single room. Number 516, for two nights.

G : Oh, and I'd like to reserve a table for dinner.

C : Yes, sir. I'll give your reservation to the restaurant. What time would you like?

Dialogue 3

O : Operator
G : Guest

O : Grand Hotel, may I help you?

G : Yeah, can I speak to Mr. Gerald Ford in room 1234?

O : Just a moment, sir. Hello? I'm sorry, sir, but Mr. Gerald Ford is not a guest of this hotel.

G : Oh, no. But he told me to call him here. Can you check again?

O : All right, sir. Sorry, sir, but there is no one here by that name in any of our rooms. What number are you calling, sir?

G : I'm calling 744－2992.

O : This is 743－2992. I'm afraid you have the wrong number.

G : Oh, I must have made a mistake. I'm sorry to have bothered you.

O : That's quite all right. Good-bye.

Dialogue 4

O : Operator
G : Guest

O : Good afternoon, operator. May I help you?

G : Yes, I'm Harry Smith, room 809. I'd like to make an international call to the U.S.A.

O : What number do you want to call?

G : Area code is 202 and the number is 756–3152.

O : Very well, Mr. Smith. Please hang up and wait in your room. I'll call you back as soon as your party is on the line.

G : Thank you.

G : Hello, Harry Smith speaking.

O : Hello, Mr. Smith. This is the operator. Your party's on the line. Go ahead, please.

G : Thanks a lot.

Dialogue 5

O : Operator
G : Guest
C : Clerk

O : Good afternoon, operator. May I help you?

G : I'd like to talk to Mr. Brown, please.

O : Wait a moment. I'm put you through to the Front Desk.

C : Good afternoon, Front Desk,. May I help you?

G : Yes, please. May I speak to Mr. Brown?

C : May I ask who's calling, please?

G : This is Philip Stewart, one of his old friends.

C : Wait a moment, Mr. Stewart. I'll see if he is in his room then I'll connect you right away.

G : Hello, John Brown speaking.

C : Good afternoon, Mr. Brown. You're wanted on the phone from your friend, Philip Stewart.

G : Thank you.

Key Expressions

I

1. Who's calling, please?
2. I'd like to place a long distance call to Daegu.
3. I'm sorry, the line is busy now.
4. Would you put me through to Mr. Brown?
5. Hold the line, please. Hang up, please.
6. Can I take a message?
7. What number are you calling?
8. He's on another phone right now.
9. I'll connect you with the bell desk.
10. Shall I ask him to call you back?
11. Would you give me a wake-up call at five?
12. Could you tell him I called, please?
13. Is there a public phone in the building?
14. Could you get me extension number 123, please?
15. The phone is out of order.

Key Expressions

II

1. I'm afraid I've got ask you to leave.
2. What nonsense is this?
3. There seems to have been a complete misunderstanding.
4. I'll sort out with the reception clerk so that you can be sure it'll never happen again.
5. We've had a complaint about the noise from your neighbor across the corridor.
6. We were having a bit of celebration.
7. The bath is damaged beyond rc pair.
8. We've got to ask you for payment towards the damages.
9. One of the members of my group was rubbed of his money.
10. Is he sure he hasn't left the things behind somewhere else?
11. He should have kept the door locked, or at least he should always shut the door.
12. If you wouldn't mind filing this form in …
13. Can I reserve a room for the day after tomorrow, please?
14. Is there much difference in price?
15. How much is that in U.S dollars?

Basic Vocabulary

switchboard[1)]
telephone operator
extension number
long distance call
overseas call
local call
station—to—station call[2)]
person—to—person call[3)]
morning call
collect call[4)]
telephone book
handset
area code[5)]
dial

circuit
night rate
time difference
confideatial[6)]
house phone
public phone
message
busy
connect
transter
notify
cable
operator[7)]
button

---

1) 전화교환기
2) 대국전화
3) 대인전화(지명전화)
4) 수신자 요금 부담 전화
5) 지역번호
6) 비밀의, 공개할 수 없다는 의미
7) 전화 교환원으로 고객과 직접 대면하지는 않으나 전화를 통한 고객응대, 메시지 전달, 정보제공, 외부로부터의 전화연결, 웨이크-업 콜 서비스 등의 역할을 한다.

❖ Unit 6 Information Service ❖

손님들에게 필요한 정보들을 친절하게 제공해야 한다.
만약 손님이 불평을 하면 고객의 입장에서 이해를 구하고 행동보다 말이 앞서서는 안된다. 사소한 불평이라도 여러 가지 기법을 사용하고 손님의 말에 귀기울여야 한다.
대부분의 고급호텔에서는 고객의 질문에 대한 대답, 문제해결 등의 업무를 수행하는 concierge를 배치하고 있다.

Section Ⅰ

Dialogue 1

B : Bellman
G : Guest

G : Excuse me, please.
Can you tell me what's on tomorrow night?

B : With pleasure, sir. I've got the program here.
Would you like to have a look at it?

G : Yes, please.

B : Look. You can see what operas, plays, musicals and operettas are on.

G : Are there any concerts? I'm very interested in classical music.

B : You are in good luck.

Dialogue 2

B : Bellman

G : Guest

G : Could you tell me the way to the nearest station?

B : Certainly, but we have a shuttle bus service every ten minutes.

G : It's alright. I'd like to walk.

B : First, go out of the hotel and walk to the right.

G : Alight, so go out of the right, and turn left and then keep going.

B : Yes, that's right, sir.

Dialogue 3

B : Bellman
G : Guest

B : Good morning, Concierge. May I help you?

G : Yes please. I need information about the Korean Folk Village. Can you tell me how I can get there?

B : Certainly, sir. I would like to suggest that you take a tour bus of travel agency.

G : How much does the bus ticket cost?

B : 10,000 won per person, sir.

G : Please give me two tickets.

B : Here you are, sir.

Dialogue 4

B : Bellman

G : Guest

B : Good afternoon, sir. May I help you?

G : Yes. I'd like this package to be delivered to Mrs. Hopkins in Room 1434

B : Certainly, sir. Is there anything valuable or breakable in the package?

G : No, there isn't.

B : I see, sir. Could you fill out this from, please?

G : Of course. Here you are.

B : Thank you, sir.

We'll deliver it to her room when she arrives.

Dialogue 5

B : Bellman

G : Guest

G : Hi, my name is Chapman in room 1343, I'm expecting a letter. Do you have anything for me?

B : Just a moment, please. I'll check it for you, sir.

Thank you for waiting. We have a letter for you, sir.

May I see your ID card, please?

G : Sure. Here you are.

B : Thank you, sir. Have a nice day.

Key Expressions

I

1. Do you have any letter for me?
2. The postal charge will be 15 dollars, sir.
3. It's on the second floor.
4. I want to send a fax, what do I have to do?
5. Go along the corridor.
6. Go straight ahead.
7. Take that escalator up one level.
8. Do you have a shuttle service?
9. How often do the buses run?
10. You can't miss it.
11. It takes about ten minutes by taxi.
12. How can I get to the souvenir shop?
13. Could you direct me to the parking lot?
14. How late is the store open, Miss?
15. How much does a subway ride cost?

Key Expressions

II

1. Can you have someone fix it?
2. My lamp seems to be broken.
3. Is the TV plugged in?
4. My TV reception seems to be no good.
5. Did you switch the power on?
6. The bathroom toilet doesn't seem to work well.
7. They will be there to check it within 5 minutes.
8. Isn't there a vending machine on my floor?
9. Do you have a converter I could use?
10. We can lend you a hair dryer instead.
11. I'm a bit tied up at the moment.
12. What time would it be convenient for you?
13. We will bring a replacement.
14. We requested some more bath towels over half an hour ago.
15. We're extremely sorry. Please forgive the delay.

Key Expressions

III

1. Could you fill the container with water?
2. Let it boil for about 7 to 8 minutes.
3. Your smoking detector is flashing.
4. Is there anything burning in your room?
5. I'm very sorry to have disturbed you.
6. You can send somebody up to make up my room.
7. These thing are for the laundry.
8. I'll let the overnight staff know.
9. How about tidying up a bit in the bathroom?
10. I'm sorry I cannot do this without the authority of Front Office.
11. I have an allergy and can't not stand feather pillows.
12. What's the exchange rate today?
13. Can I exchange this much Korean won for U.S dollars?
14. Do you cash checks here?
15. Do you want everything on one receipt?

Basic Vocabulary

subway system[1]
register[2]
lost and found[3]
lost article report[4]
information desk[5]
attendant[6]
corridor
direction
flight[7]
gymnasium
lounge
night club
cabaret

car rental
parking lot
postal charge[8]
ordinary service
quick service
tuxedo
blanket
pillow
shuttle but
tour bus
morning tour
afternoon tour
night tour

---

1) 지하철 노선
2) 등기우편(registered mail)
3) 분실물 보관소
4) 분실물 신고서
5) 투숙객 및 모든 호텔 고객에게 호텔시설 및 각종 정보를 제공해 주는 역할을 한다.
6) 관리원, 수행원, 참가자
7) 한층계, 연속된 계단
8) 우편요금

❖ Unit 7 Laundry Service ❖

호텔 세탁물 서비스는 하우스 키퍼의 영역이며 많은 시트, 타월, 식탁보 냅킨 등을 세탁한다.

세탁물 서비스는 손님들에게 세탁과 다림질 등과 같은 서비스를 신속하고 효과적으로 제공해야 한다.

Dialogue 1

C : Clerk
G : Guest

C : Laundry service, May I help you?

G : Yes, I have some shirts to be cleaned and pressed. Can you send someone over to my room?

C : May I have your name and room number, please?

G : My name is Frank Bennet, and my room number is 1516.

C : All right, sir. I'll have a valet pick them up right away.

G : All right. Thank you!

Dialogue 2

C : Clerk
G : Guest

C : Laundry service, can I help you?

G : Yes, please. I have some shirts and pants to be cleaned and pressed. Can you send someone over to my room?

C : May I have your name and room number, please?

G : My name is Philip Myers, and my room number is 814.

C : All right, sir. I'll send a valet to your room quickly.

G : I'm going out in 20 minutes.

C : I'll have him pick them up right away.

G : All right, thank you.

Dialogue 3

C : Clerk

L : Launderer

G : How much does it cost to launder my suit?

L : It depends.

But usually it's US $25.

G : Can I get it back by seven this evening if I send it now?

L : Yes. it's possible, but you have to pay a special charge for it.

G : No problem at all.

I'll pay a special charge for my suit.

L : Thank you, sir.

Dialogue 4

C : housekeeping Clerk
G : Guest

C : Housekeeping, may I help you?

G : Yes, please have a maid come up to my room eleven-fifteen(1115). The room is just in a mess.

C : Yes, sir. Is there anything else?

G : Yes, I want an extra blanket and two bath towels.

C : I'll have them sent up to your room right away, sir.

G : Could you get me a bed cover in dark purple, too?

C : I'm sorry, but we don't have that color. How about a light pink?

G : Good enough. I'll take that.

Dialogue 5

C : Clerk
G : Guest

G : I have some laundry and dry cleaning. If I send out laundry today, when can I get it back?

C : Usually you can get it back on the next day. But if you want, you can get it in the evening. If you rushed, you have to pay an extra charge.

G : There is no need to be rushed. Can I take the laundry slip?

C : Here you are.

G : One moment. I'll fill out laundry slip.

C : Very well, sir.

G : Here it is. Please check it to see whether it is correct. Is that correct?

C : Yes, perfect. When do you want it to be delivered?

G : I'd like to get it back at about 4 o'clock tomorrow afternoon.

C : OK.

Key Expressions

I

1. Housekeeping, may I help you?
2. I need these shirts cleaned.
3. I want these clothes pressed.
4. You can just give your laundry to the housemaid.
5. Don't fail to remove this stain on the jacket.
6. When can I get this laundry back?
7. When do you want to get it back?
8. They usually get back it the following day.
9. The room is just in a mess.
10. It needs cleaning.
11. Is this for washing or pressing?
12. Are you in a hurry, sir?
13. I'll go down and pick it up right away.
14. What is your purse made of?
15. I hope you will do a good job.

Key Expressions

II

1. Can you tell me how I can get there?
2. I would like to suggest that you take a tour bus of a travel agency.
3. Can you get us some tickets?
4. I'll call the box office to check if there are any tickets available for tomorrow night.
5. I'm sorry, there aren't any tickets left for tomorrow night.
6. Can you tell me what's on tomorrow night?
7. You can see what operas, play, musical and operettas are on.
8. I'm very interested in classical music.
9. I'd like to package to be delivered to Mrs. Hopkins in Room 1434
10. Is there anything valuable or breakable in the package?
11. It weighs 2 kilograms and will cost 8,500 won, please.
12. Can I charge it to my room
13. How long will it take to the States?
14. Could you leave it in my mailbox?
15. Can someone help me with it?

Basic Vocabulary

housekeeping
housekeeper
maintenance
repairman
safe
valuables
belongings
laundry
laundryman
launderer
laundry slip[1)]
ordinary service
quick services
valet[2)]
clothes repair
blanket
towel
pillow
suit
tuxedo
sheet
trousers
stain

---

1) 세탁물 전표
2) 심부름 시킨다(배달)의 의미. 호텔에서는 고객의 차량 주차대행과 세탁물 배달의 경우에 사용되는 용어(valet service)

❖ Unit 8 Banquet Service ❖

호텔의 가장 중요한 수입원 중의 하나가 음식과 음료의 판매이다. 식당은 모든 고객들에게 즐겁고 안락한 분위기를 제공해야 한다. 모든 종사자들은 예의 바르고 신속한 서비스를 제공해야 하며 상세한 메뉴 등을 숙지해야 한다.

호텔은 객실뿐만 아니라 다양한 행사를 할 수 있는 많은 공간을 가지고 있다. 연회실, 회의실, 식당 등과 같은 서비스 시설물들이 있다.

Dialogue 1

R : Banquet Receptionist
G : Guest

R : Banquet reception, may I help you?

G : Yes, please. I'd like to book a room for lunch tomorrow.

R : Yes, sir. How many people would there be?

G : Ten people, five men and five women.

R : I see. And what time will you be arriving?

G : Around eleven-thirty, I think.

R : A room for ten at eleven-thirty on Saturday. May I have your name and telephone number?

G : My name is Kim and you can get in touch with me at 745-1234.

R : Very good, Mr. Kim. What kind of function would it be?

G : Oh, it will be a birthday party in honor of Dr. Chung's 60th birthday.

R : We'll look forward to seeing you, Mr. Kim.
Good-bye.

Dialogue 2

R : Banquet Receptionist
G : Guest

R : Our reception desk is over here, sir. Let me check your things for you.

G : The party begins at ten?

R : Yes, sir. Quite a few of the guests have already arrived.

G : Can you tell me who they are?

R : They are members of the Chamber of Commerce and Industry in Taegu City.

(*Inside the garden*)

G : It's a beautiful garden, isn't it?

R : Yes, sir. It's well kept in this hotel.

G : A garden party has a charm of its own.

R : As you know, a party in the open gives a greater sense of freedom than one held in a room.

G : Outdoor parties are very nice, don't you think so?

Dialogue 3

C : Clerk
G : Guest

C : Good afternoon. May I help you?

G : Yes, I'd like see some Korean traditional variety shows if there is any around here.

C : There is a good one in the downtown. They perform everyday evening from 7 : 00.

G : Sounds fantastic. How much does it cost?

C : 35,000 Won per person including dinner, sir.

G : What about kids, do they charge the full price?

C : Children under 12 is a half price, sir.

G : Good. Would you book for my family, two adults and 3 kids, please?

C : Certainly, sir.

Dialogue 4

R : Banquet Receptionist
G : Guest

G : Excuse me.

R : Yes.

May I help you, sir?

G : I'm from New York, I'm going to Hotel Inter-Continental.

Do you have Limousine Service from here?

R : Sure.

The ticket counter for the Limousine is over there in this terminal building.

We have four different Limousine lines for the major hotels in Seoul from Kimpo International Airport.

G : How much is the bus fare?

R : It's 5000 won.

It leaves every fifteen minutes.

G : Thank you so much.

Dialogue 5

R : Banquet Receptionist
G : Guest

R : Banquet reception, may I help you?

G : Yes, can I speak to the manager, please?

R : I'm sorry, sir, he has just stepped out of the office, and he won't be back until two-thirty. Could I take a message?

G : Yes. I reserved a table for six people this evening, but I'm afraid I'll have to cancel it.

R : May I have your name, please?

G : Gerald Brown.

R : Sorry, but I didn't catch that. Could you spell it, please?

G : Brown, B—R—O—W—N.

R : Very good, Mr. Brown. I'll be sure the manager gets the message. Good-bye.

Key Expressions

I

1. What time will you be arriving?
2. How many people would there be?
3. How much per person would you like to spend?
4. Can you tell me who they are?
5. I'm afraid I'll have to cancel it.
6. I shall never forget your kindness.
7. A garden party has a charm of its own.
8. The pleasure is mine.
9. What sort of function would it be?
10. I'm sorry, I didn't catch that.
11. Can you suggest some nice place for our dinner?
12. We have a very good room available for your party.
13. I'll call you at your office when it's ready.
14. I'd like to book a room for lunch tomorrow.
15. The party begins at ten.

Key Expressions

II

1. Will you stay until then?
2. Would please inquire again tomorrow morning?
3. I'll be in the position to help you.
4. That's very kind of you.
5. Where can I park my car?
6. You can use our underground garage, it's complimentary.
7. I wish you a pleasant stay in our hotel.
8. Can you help me with this form, please?
9. I'd like to reconfirm the schedule for the period of your stay.
10. Is there any change in the number of your group?
11. I'm afraid we've had some last minute changes.
12. Any change in your schedule?
13. Did you enjoy your stay with us?
14. I'm afraid this credit card has just expired.
15. How are you going to pay, Mr. Wagner? In cash or with credit card?

Basic Vocabulary

conference[1]
banquet
reception
welcome party
farewell party
garden party
loudspeaker
microphone
tape recorder
video recorder
word processor
closed circuit TV[2]
table service
buffet service
self service
function[3]
reception
seminar
workshop
recreation
bouquet
compliments

1) 회의
2) 폐쇄 회로 TV
3) 행사

❖ Unit 9 Room Service ❖

호텔의 객실은 가장 중요한 부분 중의 하나이다. 호텔은 깨끗하고 마음에 드는 방을 손님에게 제공해야 한다.

룸메이드는 방을 깨끗이 해야하고 필요한 모든 물품들을 공급해야한다. 호텔의 크고 작음에 관계없이 객실은 항상 최상의 상태에 있어야 한다.

Section I

Dialogue 1

C : Clerk
G : Guest

C : Room Service, may I help you, sir?

G : Mr. Smith in 808.

I'd like to have some food.

C : May I take your order, sir?

G : I'd like to have fried chicken for two and two bottles of beer.

I also want a glass of orange juice and hot coffee, please.

C : Will that be all, sir?

G : Yes, that's all.

C : Thank you, sir. It'll take about ten minutes.

G : That's fine.

Dialogue 2

C : Clerk
G : Guest

C : Housekeeping. Can I help you?

G : Yes, I need my room cleaned up.

C : What's your room number, sir?

G : 1128.

C : Yes, a room maid will be there in 5 minutes.

(a little later)

C : (knocking on the door) Hello?

G : Yes, who is it?

C : Housekeeping, may I come in to make up the room?

G : Yes, please but don't touch the papers. I'm working on them.

C : Sure, sir.

Dialogue 3

W : Waiter
G : Guest

W : Room service. Can I help you?

G : Yes, we'd like to have breakfast in our room tomorrow morning.

W : May I take your order, now?

G : I need to see the menu, first.

Would you please send the menu to our room?

W : You'll find a menu in the drawer of your night table, ma'am.

G : Oh, really?

Could you wait for a minute?

Yes, I've found it.

Let's see, I think we need some time to decide.

Can I call you back in 5 minutes to order?

W : Certainly, ma'am.

Dialogue 4

C : Clerk
G : Guest

C : Room service.

G : I'd like to have lunch in my room.

C : All right, sir.
May I have your room number?

G : Room 518, and I want a club sandwich on rye with extra mustard.

C : OK. Anything else?

G : Oh, please hold the mayonnaise.
I'm allergic to it.

C : Very well, sir.
Anything to drink?

G : Yes, a cup of coffee with cream, no sugar, please.

C : What time would you like it to be ready, sir?

G : At one o'clock.

C : All right.
Thank you for your order, sir.

Dialogue 5

C : Room Service Clerk

G : Guest

C : (*Knocking on the door*) Room service!

G : Come in.

The door isn't locked.

C : Good morning, ma'am.

Your breakfast is ready.

G : Thank you.

Please put everything on this table.

C : I'm afraid this table is too small.

I'll go and get a large one.

G : All right.

And please keep the bacon and eggs covered.

C : Yes, ma'am.

Key Expressions

I

1. Room service, May I help you?
2. What time would you like it served?
3. What would you like to order?
4. The room service is available 24 hours a day.
5. We'll send it up in about 30 minutes.
6. Would you please sign this slip?
7. Where would you like to eat?
8. It won't take too long.
9. We have a "no tipping" policy here.
10. Enjoy your dinner.
11. I've brought the dinner you ordered.
12. May I have dinner delivered to my room?
13. I want to keep the tea hot.
14. Something is wrong with the T.V set.
15. We'll call you back right away.

Basic Vocabulary

room service[1]	chambermaid
maid	blouse
laundry	skirt
dry-cleaning	dress
night table	shirt
drawer	undershirt
socket	underpants
cord	trousers
plug	hamburger
electric percolator[2]	cheeseburger
pitcher	fishburger

---

1) 음식 및 음료의 객실 배달서비스
2) 여과 장치가 있는 커피나 홍차를 끓이는 도구

❖ Unit 10 Cashier Service ❖

호텔의 캐셔는 손님과의 관계에서 중요한 역할을 하고 있다. 퇴숙절차는 손님들이 호텔 이용시에 발생된 불편함 등을 말할 수 있는 기회가 되며 호텔 측에서는 손님에게 감사를 전할 수 있는 마지막 기회이기 때문이다.

Dialogue 1

C : Front Clerk
G : Guest

C : Good afternoon, front desk.

May I help you, sir?

G : This is Mrs. Kim in room 1314.

I'd like to check out tomorrow morning.

C : What time would you like to check out, ma'am?

G : At six, very early in the morning.

I should be at the airport by 6 : 30 a.m.

C : Your bill will be ready by five tomorrow morning.

G : I'd like to know the total amount now if it's possible.

C : Wait a moment, please.

Dialogue 2

C : Cashier
G : Guest

C : May I help you, sir?

G : Yes. I'd like to change U.S dollars into Korean money.

What's the rate today?

C : Today's exchange rate is one-thousand-two-hundred-won for one dollar.

How much do you want to change?

G : Two-hundred-dollars.

C : How do you want it, sir?

G : I need all ten-thousand-won notes.

Dialogue 3

C : Cashier

G : Guest

C : Good afternoon, ma'am, can I help you?

G : Good afternoon.

I'd like to cash this check into Korean won.

C : Just a moment, ma'am.

Today's exchange rate is one-thousand-two-hundred-ninety-two-won for one U.S dollar. How much would you like to change, ma'am?

G : Please give me a change for one hundred dollars.

C : Would you fill out this form and show me your passport, please?

G : Here you are.

Dialogue 4

C : Front Clerk

G : Guest

C : Good morning.

May I help you, sir?

G : I'm going to leave now.

Can you make out my bill?

C : May I have your name and room number, please?

G : John Bennet, 1487.

C : It comes to 305,000 won, sir.

How would you like to pay, sir?

G : I'd like to pay by credit card.

C : Very well, would you give me your credit card and passport, please?

G : Here you are.

C : I hope you enjoyed stay here.

Dialogue 5

C : Cashier
G : Guest

C : Did you enjoy your meal, sir?

G : Yes, I did.
Can I pay by check?

C : Oh, I'm sorry, sir, but we don't accept personal checks.

G : All right, then, I'll pay in cash.

C : Thank you anyway, sir, but we have a no tipping policy.
Every tip is included in a ten percent service charge added to your bill.

G : OK. That's fine.
What does it come to?

C : It comes to 28,000 won.

G : Then, here is 30,000 won.

C : Your change is 2,000 won and here's your receipt.
Thank you very much, sir.

Key Expressions

I

1. What does this mean?

2. Do you take credit card?

3. Could you sign here, please?

4. Please keep this copy of the form.

5. We'll give you the change in local currency.

6. I'll just put it through the computer again.

7. I'm afraid this credit card has already expired.

8. I'll check it for you.

9. What's your room number?

10. How much do you want to change?

11. I'd like to change U.S. dollars into Korean money.

12. I'd like to cash this check into Korean won.

13. What is the rate of exchange today?

14. That's for the phone call you made.

15. Your room charges were prepaid through your travel agency.

Key Expressions

II

1. Could I pay by check, then?
2. I'm afraid we wouldn't normally accept a check without a valid check guarantee card.
3. If you'd like to wait a moment, we'll put a telephone call through to your bank.
4. I'll write out a slip for you and give you a receipt.
5. Would you like me to explain any items?
6. I did get some laundry done.
7. I'd like to pay my bill.
8. Are you leaving today?
9. Are you the right person to discuss about it?
10. I'll connect you to our manager who would be the right person to discuss about it.
11. Have you any really special accommodation we can offer them?
12. We will give VIP guests special treatment when necessary.
13. The fax you sent hasn't reached us yet.
14. I'm afraid we are full up for tonight, sir.
15. Would you like the breakdown of the bill?

Key Expressions

III

1. Can I settle my bill?
2. I'll get your statement right away.
3. How are you going to pay, sir? In cash or with a credit card?
4. Let me check it out first.
5. What's this amount for?
6. Could you go through it item by item and explain it all?
7. Can I pay with credit card?
8. We have to hurry up little bit to catch a plane.
9. I'll have to give you part of it in dollars.
10. Here is your change.
11. I'd like to settle my bill, please.
12. I'll draw up your bill for you.
13. Would you mind letting me have a look at it?
14. Do you change money here?
15. I'd like to pay my bills in cash and charge the rest of it on my credit card.

Basic Vocabulary

note[1)]
bill
safe deposit box[2)]
page[3)]
service charge[4)]
traveler's check[5)]
denomination[6)]
currency[7)]
Korean won
Japanese yen
US dollar
British pound
Russian rouble
Mexican peso
foreign exchange
exchange rate
money changer
black market
credit card
charged card[8)]
cash
personal check
monetary amount[9)]
French franc
German mark

---

1) 지폐, 화폐 어음, 증권
2) 호텔 안전 금고
3) paging service
4) 봉사료
5) 여행자 수표
6) 액면금액
7) 통화, 화폐
8) 신용지불카드
9) 금액

❖ Unit 11 Check-out ❖

숙박한 호텔에서 숙박료를 지급하고 퇴숙하는 것이며 손님들에게 신속하게 처리해주어야 한다. 손님들의 이름, 호실, 요금 등을 요령 있게 알도록 하며 손님들의 요금 지불 방법을 물어서 처리하면 된다.

Dialogue 1

C : Clerk
G : Guest

C : Good morning, sir.
What can I do for you, sir?
G : I'd like to pay my bill.
I'm Kim in room 1145.
C : Your bill comes to $80.
How would you like to pay, sir?
G : Can I use my credit card here?
C : Sure, sir.
G : How about Master Card?
C : It's O.K. May I take a print of your card?
G : Of course. Here you are.
C : Would you please sign here, please?
G : All right. Here it is.
C : Thank you, sir. Here are your card and receipt, sir.
I sincerely wish you have a nice trip.
G : Thanks a lot. See you again.

Dialogue 2

C : Cashier
G : Guest

C : Good morning, Mr. Crooney. May I help you?

G : I'm ready to check out. Room 1318.

C : Very well, sir. I'll print out your bill right away. Just a moment, please.

G : Would you please hurry? I have a plane to catch in 2 hours.

C : All right, sir.

G : Sorry to make you rush.

C : No problem. sir. Would you please give us your next destination? Just in case we need to forward your letters or any messages.

G : Oh, very good. Here it is.

Dialogue 3

C : Clerk
G : Guest

C : Good morning, may I help you?

G : Yes, please. When is your check-out time?

C : One o'clock p.m. sir. Are you checking out today?

G : Yes, I am. But my flight is not until this evening. Could I stay in the room until 6 : 00 tonight?

C : I'm sorry, sir, but if you don't check out by one p.m., then you'll have to pay one-day extra charge.

G : Oh, no, I can't afford that. Can't you make a special arrangement only for me?

C : Sorry, sir, but it's our hotel's rule. I'm afraid I can't break it, You'd better speak to the manager about it if you wish.

G : All right, I'll do that. Thank you very much.

C : You're welcome, sir.

Dialogue 4

C : Clerk
G : Guest

C : Here is your bill, sir.

G : Oh, thank you. Let's have a look at it now. Goodness! It's a lot more than I expected.

C : Would you like me to explain any items, sir?

G : Yes, just a moment, what's this charge for 8,000 won marked 'L'?

C : 'L' is a charge for a long distance telephone call, sir. Did you make a telephone call that night?

G : Yes! I remember now. Gosh, we must have talked for a long time!

Dialogue 5

C : Clerk
G : Guest

C : Good morning. May I help you?

G : Yes. Will you send someone to take my luggage to the front? I'm going to check out at 11 : 00.

C : Yes, sir. The bellman will be there in a minute.

G : Will you call me a taxi? I have to arrive at the airport by one o'clock. I'd better hurry.

C : Yes, sir. I'll let you know when your taxi is ready.

G : Thank you.

C : You're welcome, sir. Did you enjoy your staying at our hotel?

G : Sure. I will come here again when I visit Korea.

Key Expressions

I

1. I'd like to check out now.
2. May I have your room number, please?
3. Are you checking out today?
4. Would you like me to explain any items?
5. I'm afraid this credit card has expired.
6. There will be a few other items to add today.
7. Would you please tell us your next destination?
8. I'll take good care of it for you.
9. Let's have a look at it now.
10. I'm afraid I cannot break the rule.
11. I suppose the bill must be right.
12. This is the amount up to this time.
13. I hope we'll see you again.
14. Have a pleasant trip.
15. Please come again.

Basic Vocabulary

check out time
check guarantee card[1)]
bill[2)]
individual bill[3)]
accommodation[4)]
service charge[5)]
dis bursement[6)]
value added tax(VAT)[7)]
change
coupon
expiry
cover charge[8)]
receipt
identification card(ID)[9)]
next destination[10)]
passport
account
arrangement[11)]
special bus[12)]
airport bus
extra charge
personal check

---

1) 고객이 개인 수표를 사용할 때 이를 증명하는 은행에서 발급한 신용카드
2) 계산서
3) 단체 투숙객들 중에서 개인이 각자 사용하는 요금 청구서
4) 숙박료
5) 봉사료
6) 지출금, 지불금
7) 부가가치세
8) 봉사료
9) 신분증명서
10) 다음 행선지
11) 배려
12) charter

Part Ⅱ

❖ Unit 1 Greeting ❖

Section A

A : Hi, Jim. It's been a long time. Where have you been?

B : I've been to Europe during last summer vacation.

A : That sounds fantastic! How's the travel?

B : It couldn't be better. I visited a lot of tourist attractions and met various people from different countries.

A : Did you take a picture a lot?

B : Yes, indeed. Why don't you drop by my office when you're free? We can talk and look at pictures together.

A : I sure will.

Section B

A : Hello, Mike.

B : Hi, Archie, how are you?

A : I'm barely making it. How about you?

B : So far so good. What's the matter? You look really depressed.

A : Well, actually I got a bad grade in Tourism English.

B : I'm sorry to hear that.

A : I should have studied a lot.

B : Are you going to be okay? Is there anything I can do for you?

A : No. There's nothing any body can do.

B : Don't be so hard on yourself. It happens to everyone and you can get a good grade in next semester.

A : Thanks. I really appreciate your advice.

Section C

A : Hello, Roger. How have you been?

B : Fine, Henry. Have you heard the news?

A : About what?

B : I'm going to the United States.

A : That's wonderful. When do you leave?

B : The day after tomorrow.

A : Do you have anything you need?

B : Oh, yes. I've always wanted to go, but now I'm wondering if I'll get along all right.

A : It will be fine. You may have trouble at first, though.

B : Do you mean the trouble with the language?

A : Yes, with the language. And probably with the food, too.

B : I shouldn't have too much trouble with English. I've been studying English for years.

A : Yes, but English here and English there are two different things.

B : A week from now, I'll know.

A : Let me know all about your adventures.

B : I'll write as often as I can. Well, I have to go now, Henry.

A : Have a good trip.

❖ Unit 2 Daily Life ❖

Section A

A : Where are you going, Bob?

B : Downtown. I have to run some errands.

A : I have to go on errands, too. May I come with you?

B : Of course. I'd be glad to have you.

A : What do you have to do?

B : I have to the laundry. I have to buy a present, too.

A : I have to go to the laundry, too.

B : OK. Wait a minute. I forgot my money. I'll have to run in the house and get some money. I'll be with you in a minute.

A : I wonder who he's going to buy a present for. My birthday isn't until next month. Maybe he's going to buy my present early.

B : Hi. Let's go. I think I'll buy the present first.

A : Don't you want me to go with you?

B : Yes, I do. You can help me.

A : Do you want me to help you select a gift for me?

B : No, not for you, Kitty. Today is my father's birthday. I want to get him a new tie.

A : Oh, I'm sorry.

Section B

A : Hi, Mark. Are you ready to go jogging?

B : Hi, Jerry. I'm almost ready. I was taking a shower. I haven't finished getting dressed yet. Where are we going to jog today?

A : I don't know. It's up to you.

B : Okay. Say, we've never gone down to the lake.

A : Oh, that's quite a long distance.

B : It's about twenty miles.

A : I've jogged twenty miles before. How about you, Mark?

B : I haven't gone that far before. We're both in good shape, though. We should be able to make it.

A : I think so, too. How much weight have you lost recently?

B : Well, I've lost about fifteen pounds since last March. Can you believe it, Jerry?

A : That's really good for only three months. How do you feel?

B : I feel great. I've and much more energy recently. I've been able to get more work done, too.

Section C

A : George, have you read the newspaper yet?

B : No, I haven't. Why?

A : There's an advertisement in it. I'm sure it would interest you. There's a new clothing store in town.

B : Have you been there yet, Martha?

A : No, not yet. I need a hat, thought. I haven't bought a new hat for two years.

B : I've worn this same suit for three years. I haven't bought any clothes for a long time. Let's go tomorrow, shall we?

A : OK. We'll go right after work.

B : Say, here's another interesting story in the newspaper.

A : What is it?

B : It says that Huh Young-ho is returning from the South Pole. It also says that he has made some important discoveries.

A : I wonder what thery are.

B : I'm wondering, too.

Section D

A : Good evening, sir. May I help you?

B : Yes, please. Thirty-five adults for "The Titanic" for the twelve-thirty show, please.

A : I'm sorry, but the twelve-thirty show has just been sold out.

B : Oh, really? What about the next show?

A : How about the five o'clock show, sir?

B : That's fine. Thirty-five adults, please. How much is it?

A : Seven fifty each. The total amount is U$262.5, sir.

B : It looks strange. As you can see here, it says only four dollars each.

A : That's only for the matinees, the shows starting before three o'clock, sir.

B : Oh, I see. Thanks a lot.

A : You're welcome, sir. Enjoy your time.

Section E

A : One adult and two children for "Home Alone 3", please.

B : I'm sorry, but the show for today has been slod out.

A : Oh, really? Then, how about "Beauty and the Beast"?

B : All right. We have some tickets for the show.

A : One adult and two kids for the one o'clock show, please.

B : Fifteen dollars, please.

A : O.K. Here is twenty dollars.

B : Thank you. Here is your change, five dollars.

A : Thanks a lot.

B : Have a nice time.

A : May I help you, ma'am?

B : Yes. I'd like to have two hamburgers, please.

Section F

A : With everything on it, ma'am?

B : Yes, please.

A : Anything to drink, ma'am?

B : Can I have a coke and a bottle of mineral water?

A : What size of coke would you like, ma'am?

B : Small size, please.

A : Will that be all, ma'am?

B : Well, popcorn, please.

A : What about the popcorn, buttered or plain?

B : Extra butter, please.

A : Thirteen twenty-five, please.

B : Here you are.

❖ Unit 3 Time and Weather ❖

Section A

A : Peter, are you going to play tennis today?

B : I don't know. It looks like rain.

A : Did you hear a weather report?

B : No, I didn't.

A : Let's do something else. I don't want to play tennis if it looks like rain.

B : Look at it rain.

A : Yes, it's a good thing we didn't try to play tennis. There's lightning, too.

B : Yes, and listen to that thunder! It's a thunderstorm.

A : Better turn on the light. It's setting dark in here.

B : OK. I'll turn it on.

Section B

A : How's the weather?

B : It's cloudy and windy.

A : I wish it would rain. We haven't had rain for a month.

B : The weather man says we're going to have some rain late this eventing.

A : That's good news. Did weather man say it's going to rain tomorrow, too?

B : Well, according to the weather forecast, it'll be raining until the end of this weekend.

Section C

A : How do you spend your free time?

B : I usually listen to music when I have a free time.

A : What kind of music do you like?

B : I like jazz. How about you?

A : Well, I like pop music.

B : Who's your favorite singer?

A : I like Simon & Garfunkel.

Section D

A : The weather is getting colder these days I guess it's really winter now.

B : I hate cold weather. I can't wait until spring comes.

A : So do I. I'm getting tired of this weather.

B : Let's go to play tennis with me this afternoon.

A : That's sounds great. What will the weather be like this afternoon?

B : According to the weather forecast, it'll be fine this afternoon but it'll be snowing tomorrow.

A : By the way, won't it be a little too cold for outdoor tennis?

B : Come on, it should be just right.

Section E

A : Hi, Jim. How have you been?

B : I've been fine, thanks.

A : What do you usually do on weekend?

B : I play tennis with my friends.

A : Do you play tennis well?

B : Well, I think I'm a pretty good player.

A : Why not. I haven't been getting enough exercise lately.

B : You need to work on developing your physical strength. Why don't you play tennis with me?

A : Why not?

B : I'd like 5×75, double prints, too please.

A : And when would you like them by?

B : How about the day after tomorrow noon?

A : Okay, I'll see you then.

Section F

A : Are you the new front desk clerk?

B : That's right. I'm the new employee.

A : Have you worked in a hotel before?

B : No, it's all new to me.

A : Where were you working before you got this job?

B : I worked at the travel agency.

A : How did you like it?

B : It's great. I traveled many countries.

Section G

A : Hello, this is Doo Seuck Song. May I speak to Bob Smith?

B : Speaking.

A : Hi, Bob. I'm calling to ask if you'd like to go fishing.

B : That sounds great. When can we meet?

A : Is four o'clock on Saturday OK?

B : That'll be fine. Where shall we meet?

A : Let's meet at the Express Bus Terminal.

B : OK. I'll see you then. Thank you for calling.

Section H

A : Hello. May I help you?

B : I'd like to get this film developed.

A : Sure. Would you like glossy or studio finish?

B : I'd like glossy, please.

A : What size would you like 3×55 or 5×75?

❖ Unit 4 Telephone ❖

Section A

A : Hi, Yum.

B : Hi, soonja. I'm glad you called. Will you hold on a moment?

A : Yes, of course I will.

B : Thanks. I had to turn down the radio.

A : Your voice doesn't sound good, Yum. Did you get sick?

B : Yes, I did. Last night I started feeling bad.

A : That's too bad. Were you at work today? I didn't see you.

B : No, I wasn't. I relaxed at home instead.

Section B

A : This is Cho ho Industry.

May I help you?

B : Yes. This is Mr. Brown speaking.

May I speak to Mr. Lee, Young-jae the president?

A : Hold on, please.

He's on another line?

B : May I leave a message?

A : Certainly, sir.

B : Would you have him call me back?

He has my phone number.

A : Certainly, sir.

I'll give your message to him.

Thank you for calling.

Section C

A : This is the secretary of Sam Sung.
May I help you, sir?

B : May I speak to Mr. Pak?

A : I'm sorry, but he went to L.A on business.

B : When do you expect him back?

A : He will be back in about two weeks.
May I take your message?

B : This is very urgent.
How can I get in touch with him?

A : May I ask who's calling?

B : My name is Bill Johnson.

A : You can reach him by calling 8616-3916 in L.A, USA.

B : Thank you for your help.

A : Thank you for calling.

Section D

A : Hello, May I help you?

B : May I speak to Mr. Cho?

A : I'm sorry, but he is not in.

B : When is he expected to be back?

A : He'll be back by one.
May I take your message?

B : Would you have him return my call?

A : Does he have your phone number?

B : Yes. he does.

A : I'll tell him to call you back.

B : Thank you for your help.

Section E

A : Golden Travel Agent. May I help you?

B : Yes, I'd like to speak to Mr. david.

A : I'm sorry. He's not at his desk right now.

B : When do you expect him back?

A : I'm not sure, but in about half an hour or so.
Would you like to leave a message?

B : Yes. This is Kim from Seoul Tourist Company.
I want to talk over our itinerary in Los Angeles.
I'm staying at the Grand Hotel in Korea Town.
Room number, 725 and phone number, 213-375-1189.

A : All right, Mr. Kim.
I'll have him call back to you right away.

B : Thank you very much.

A : You're welcome. Good-bye.

Section F

A : Orient Tourist Company. Can I help you?

B : Yes, please. I'd like to speak to Ms. Lisa Diamond.

A : She is not in at the moment.

I'm sorry, but who is calling, please?

B : This is Charles Cho from Seoul Travel.

This morning I called for her.

When do you expect her back?

A : I'm sorry, sir. I'm not sure.

May I take a message, sir?

B : Yes, please.

Could you ask her to call me back, please?

A : Certainly, sir.

May I have your phone number?

B : It's 213-838-5523.

A : I'm sorry, but could you spell your name?

B : It's Charles … C.H.A.R.L.E.S.

A : Thank you, sir.

I'll give her the message.

B : Thanks a lot. Good-bye.

Section G

A : Operator. May I halp you?

B : Yes, please.

I'd like to make a collect call to Seoul.

I want to speak to Mr. Park.

Phone number in Korea is 82-2-533-1257.

A : O.K., sir.

May I have your name, please?

B : Michael Choi. The last name is Choi.

A : All right, Mr. Choi. Hold on a second.

Hello, this is United States.

I have a collect call from Mr. Choi.

Would you like to accept the charges?

(Voice from Seoul : Yes.)

Mr. Choi, go ahead.

B : Thanks a lot.

❖ Unit 5 Trip ❖

Section A

A : Hello, Roger. How have you been?

B : Fine, Henry. Have you heard the news?

A : About what?

B : I'm going to the United States.

A : That's wonderful. When do you leave?

B : The day after tomorrow.

A : Do you have anything you need?

B : Oh, yes. I've always wanted to go, but now I'm wondering if I'll get along all right.

A : It will be fine. You may have trouble at first, though.

B : Do you mean the trouble with the language?

A : Yes, with the language. And probably with the food, too.

B : I shouldn't have too much trouble with English. I've been studying English for years.

A : Yes, but English here and English there are two different things.

B : A week from now, I'll know.

A : Let me know all about your adventures.

B : I'll write as often as I can. Well, I have to go now, Henry.

A : Have a good trip.

Section B

A : Good morning, sir. May I help you?

B : I want to buy a copy of the News-week.

A : Do you want to buy an English-edition?

B : Yes, of course.

A : I'm sorry, but it doesn't come out yet.

B : When can I bye it?

A : Perhaps, in a few days, sir.

B : Would you please keep one for me.

With pleasure, sir. Is there anything else you want now?

B : Do you have a map of this city?

A : Yes, we have the best one. Here it is.

B : It seems good. I'll take this.

Section C

A : May I help you, sir?

B : Yes, please. These are my bags. Please take these to the taxi stand.

A : Very well, sir. How many baggages do you have?

B : Two. I'll take one myself. What's the price for each piece of baggage?

A : Two dollars, please.

B : That's OK. Where is the nearest money exchange?

A : Go straight and you'll find it on the right.

B : Please let's go there and then I'd like to change money.

A : That's good. First go there and then to the taxi stand.

B : Thank you very much.

❖ Unit 6 Getting Directions ❖

Section A

A : Hello, Hilton hotel front desk. May I help you?

B : Could you give me directions?

A : Where're you coming from?

B : At the Kimpo International Airport.

A : You can either take a taxi or a shuttle bus.

B : Where can I take a shuttle bus?

A : You can take a shuttle bus out of the airport.

Section B

A : Excuse me, where can I get a taxi?

B : Right outside the airport. By the way, where are you going?

A : I'm going to the Sofitel Hotel.

B : Why don't you take a shuttle bus to the Sofitel Hotel?

A : Is there a shuttle bus to the Sofitel Hotel?

B : Yes. Go right through those doors. It's on the left.

A : Thank you very much.

B : Any time. Enjoy your trip.

Section C

A : May I help you?

B : Maybe you can. I'm looking for the Parkview Motel. I have to meet a friend of mine there.

A : Let me see, the Parkview Motel. Well, it must be near the park.

B : Yes, I think so, too.

A : The park is about a mile from here.

B : I guess I should take a bus to go there. If I don't, I'll be late.

A : I think it's a good idea that you should take a taxi. There aren't many buses at this time of the day.

B : Would you show me where to get a taxi?

A : Yes, I'd be glad to. Over there.

B : Thank you very much.

A : I'd get a cab for you if I had more time, but this is my lunch hour. I have to get back to my office.

B : Oh, that's all right. You've been very helpful. Thank you.

Section D

A : Excuse me, would you tell me how to get to the American Embassy?

B : Sure, go 3 blocks up Main Street and take a left, and go west 2 blocks past the park. You can't miss it.

A : Do you happen to know their business hours?

B : They're open from 9 a.m. to 4 : 30 p.m. Monday though Friday.

A : Thank you so much.

B : You're very welcome.

Section E

A : Hi, Mark! What's new?

B : I got tickets to the big football game on Sunday!

A : Wow, that was lucky!

B : Yes, but I've never driven to the football stadium. I always rode with someone else. On Sunday, I'm the driver!

A : I can give you some simple directions. I've driven there often. First, take the Freeway—Interstate Fifteen—and head south.

B : OK, south on Interstate Fifteen. Then what?

A : You'll need to watch the signs. After you pass Adams Drive, get into the right lane.

B : Fine—I get into the right lane after Adams Drive.

Section F

A : Taxi!

B : Good evening, sir. Where to?

A : Sofitel Hotel, please.

B : Very well, sir. Is this your first time to visit Korea?

A : Yes, it is. And I'm here on vacation.

B : How long are you going to stay?

A : A couple of weeks. Where would you like to recommend for sightseeing?

B : I'd like to recommend Mr. Sorak.

Section G

A : Excuse me. Could you tell me the way to Seoul Hotel?

B : Take the first right, go over train tracks, then take the second left, go past the cinema. Seoul Hotel is next to cinema on the right.

A : How long does it take to get there?

B : It's fifteen minutes on foot.
You'd better take a taxi.

A : Thank you for your kindness.

B : Any time.

A : Excuse me, sir. I'm trying to find the Y.M.C.A. Hotel. Can you tell me how to get to?

B : Walk to the corner. Then make a left turn, then walk two blocks to the traffic light. Make another left to the Y.M.C.A. Hotel.

A : I really appreciate your help.

B : No problem. Good luck.

Section H

A : Excuse me.

B : Yes. What can I do for you?

A : Where can I find the nearest Tourism Office around here?

B : Well, when you leave this building, please turn right on 5th Avenue. Then you'll see the park on the right and City Hall on the left.

A : City Hall on the left side?

Avenue. Tourism Office is the third building on the right, acorss from National Museum.

B : It's my pleasure. Have a pleasant trip.

Section I

A : Excuse me.

Could you show me the way to Hertz Rent-a-Car?

B : You're looking for the rental agency?

A : Yes, I'm going to rent a car.

B : Oh, I see. Please turn right when you leave here.

Then go straight on this street for two blocks.

A : Let's see. make a right turn and go two blocks?

B : That's right. Then you can find a fire station.

You can find it in front of the fire station.

It's very easy for you to find it.

You can't miss much.

A : Thank you very much.

B : It's my pleasure. Have a nice day.

Section J

A : Excuse me. Could you give us directions to Paul Revere's house from the hotel?

B : Certainly. Do you intend to walk or to drive?

A : We'd like to walk if it's not too far.

B : It's about twenty, twenty-five minutes away. Do you have a map?

A : Yes, here it is.

B : Okay. We're right here, at the corner of Treemont Street and Bedford street. Walk north along Treemont. You'll be on Boston's Freedom Trail.

A : Oh, Yes. I see it marked here on the map.

B : Continue on Treemont until it ends at Center Plaza.

A : Do we take Clinton Street?

B : Yes. For one block.

A : Great. Thanks very much.

❖ Unit 7 Experience ❖

Section A

A : What's the matter, Frank?

B : Oh, Jane. Nothing much. I'm a little disappointed, that's all.

A : Why?

B : My vacation is about over. I haven't done anything.

A : Nothing at all?

B : Well, let's see. I've repaired my car. I've painted the house. I've built a garage.

A : Is that all?

B : No. I've worked in the garden.

Section B

A : Excuse me. I want a computer. Would you show me around?

B : With pleasure.

A : Recently many offices are computerized.

B : Certainly, sir. It is said that the age of computopia has come.

A : Many friends of mine have computers, and my seven year old son wants to do the computer games.

B : Many customers arc showing interests in computers.

A : I know nothing about computers at all.

B : Computers are easy to handle, and they're very interesting.

A : How long does it take us to learn the computer?

B : Well, it depends on the model yu choose. For the beginner, a simple and easy one is recommendable.

A : Isn't this model complicated?

B : No. It will take you about two hours to learn the basic knowledge necessary to operate computer.

Section C

My family consists of just four members, my parents, my brother, and me. My brother is five years older than I am. He's thirty-seven, and he's a mailman in San Francisco. He's been a mailman since he was eighteen years old, so he's been doing that for nineteen years. He decided to become a mailman when he got out of high school. He know he didn't want to go on to college. He had never liked school, and he also know that he wouldn't be happy at a job that kept him inside. So, the only thing he could think of that would earn him a living and keep him outside was becoming a mailman. So, he took an examination and did very well on it, and two weeks later, began working as a mailman. He's been doing that ever since.

Part Ⅲ

Unit 1

Unit 2

Unit 3

❖ Unit 1 ❖

1

1. Good morning, sir. May I help you?
2. Can I stay at your hotel tonight?
3. How long will you be staying here?
4. What kind of room would you like, sir?
5. We are booked up for tonight.
6. We have a double room available for that period.
7. Can I make a reservation a single room tonight?
8. Would you please tell me your expected arrival time?
9. What day will you arrive on?
10. How about a suite room instead of a double room?
11. Please givc me the reservation desk.
12. The rate will be 150 dollars a night including breakfast.
13. What would the charge be?
14. I'd like to reserve a room for two adults and a child.
15. We look forward to seeing you.

2

1. Would you please register?
2. Would you fill in this registration card?
3. How many rooms do you need?
4. How many people are there in your party?
5. What's your family name?
6. What's your nationality?
7. May I see your passport, please?
8. Where was the passport issued?
9. Where are you going after this?
10. How do you spell your name, sir?
11. Shall I find another hotel for you?
12. When did you make reservation?
13. Is there a special rate by the week?
14. Can I extend my stay for anther night?
15. I hope you will enjoy your stay in our hotel.

3

1. May I help you with your baggage?
2. How many bags do you have in all?
3. Thank you. But no tipping is our pride.
4. Mind your hands in the revolving door.
5. There are no regular taxis here now.
6. I will show you to your room.
7. Any other baggage coming, sir?
8. Where shall I put your baggage, sir?
9. The stationery and hotel brochures are here.
10. You'll be charged for what you drink.
11. Please make use of it anytime.
12. Would you like me to reserve a table for you?
13. How do I call the room service?
14. Does the room door lock itself?
15. If you require other services, just contact No. 2 bell desk.

4

1. Who's calling, please?
2. I'd like to place a long distance call to Daegu.
3. I'm sorry, the line is busy now.
4. Would you put me through to Mr. Brown?
5. Hold the line, please. Hang up, please.
6. Can I take a message?
7. What number are you calling?
8. He's on another phone right now.
9. I'll connect you with the bell desk.
10. Shall I ask him to call you back?
11. Would you give me a wake-up call at five?
12. Could you tell him I called, please?
13. Is there a public phone in the building?
14. Could you get me extension number 123, please?
15. The phone is out of order.

5

1. Do you have any letter for me?
2. The postal charge will be 15 dollars, sir.
3. It's on the second floor.
4. I want to send a fax, what do I have to do?
5. Go along the corridor.
6. Go straight ahead.
7. Take that escalator up one level.
8. Do you have a shuttle service?
9. How often do the buses run?
10. You can't miss it.
11. It takes about ten minutes by taxi.
12. How can I get to the souvenir shop?
13. Could you direct me to the parking lot?
14. How late is the store open, Miss?
15. How much does a swbway ride cost?

6

1. Housekeeping, may I help you?
2. I need these shirts cleaned.
3. I want these clothes pressed.
4. You can just give your laundry to the housemaid.
5. Don't fail to remove this stain on the jacket.
6. When can I get this laundry back?
7. When do you want to get it back?
8. They usually get back it the following day.
9. The room is just in a mess.
10. It needs cleaning.
11. Is this for washing or pressing?
12. Are you in a hurry, sir?
13. I'll go down and pick it up right away.
14. What is your purse made of?
15. I hope you will do a good job.

7

1. What time will you be arriving?
2. How many people would there be?
3. How much per person would you like to spend?
4. Can you tell me who they are?
5. I'm afraid I'll have to cancel it.
6. I shall never forget your kindness.
7. A garden party has a charm of its own.
8. The pleasure is mine.
9. What sort of function would it be?
10. I'm sorry, I didn't catch that.
11. Can you suggest some nice place for our dinner?
12. We have a very good room available for your rarty.
13. I'll call you at your office when it's ready.
14. I'd like to book a room for lunch tomorrow.
15. The party begins at ten.

8

1. Room service, May I help you?
2. What time would you like it served?
3. What would you like to order?
4. The room service is available 24 hours a day.
5. We'll send it up in about 30 minutes.
6. Would you please sign this slip?
7. Where would you like to eat?
8. It won't take too long.
9. We have a "no tipping" policy here.
10. Enjoy your dinner.
11. I've brought the dinner you ordered.
12. May I have dinner delivered to my room?
13. I want to keep the tea hot.
14. Something is wrong with the T.V. set.
15. We'll call you back right away.

9

1. What does this mean?
2. Do you take credit card?
3. Could you sign here, please?
4. Please keep this copy of the form.
5. We'll give you the change in local currency.
6. I'll just put it through the computer again.
7. I'm afraid this credit card has already expired.
8. I'll check it for you.
9. What's your room number?
10. How much do you want to change?
11. I'd like to change U.S. dollars into Korean money.
12. I'd like to cash this check into Korean won.
13. What is the rate of exchange today?
14. That's for the phone call you made.
15. Your room charges were prepaid through your travel agency.

10

1. I'd like to check out now.
2. May I have your room number, please?
3. Are you checking out today?
4. Would you like me to explain any items?
5. I'm afraid this credit card has expired.
6. There will be a few other items to add today.
7. Would you please tell us your next destination?
8. I'll take good care of it for you.
9. Let's have a look at it now.
10. I'm afraid I cannot break the rule.
11. I suppose the bill must be right.
12. This is the amount up to this time.
13. I hope we'll see you again.
14. Have a pleasant trip.
15. Please come again.

11

1. May I give you a wine list, sir?
2. What kind of vegetable would you like?
3. How would you like your eggs?
4. What would you like to drink?
5. How would you like to steak?
6. Rare (Medium, Well-done), please.
7. Would you like some more coffee?
8. Would you like a high chair for your little boy?
9. We reserved a bable this morning.
10. How many are there in your party?
11. Do you have reservation?
12. I'll show you seats.
13. Come this way, plcase.
14. How large is your aprty?
15. We'll be expecting you.

12

1. What kind of dressing for your salad?
2. Here is your table.
3. May I take your coat, ma'am?
4. Would you like to sit outside, sir?
5. Would you like something to drink before your meal?
6. What will you have for dessert?
7. Thank you for your order.
8. Shall I remove your plate?
9. It's including 10% service charge and 10% tax.
10. We accept all credit card.
11. What kind of juice would you like?
12. What kind of cereal would you like?
13. Do you have a table for two?
14. Would you like anything else?
15. I'll bring them right away, sir.

13

1. Can I have a table by the window?
2. Please let me see the munu.
3. Please rush my order.
4. make sure it's good and crisp.
5. Make my toast light.
6. This is not what I ordered.
7. Which fruit would you like?
8. Would you like a high chair for your little girl?
9. What would you like your eggs served with?
10. May I take your order?
11. I'll have my eggs scrambled.
12. What kind of soup would you like?
13. I'll show you how to use chopstics.
14. What's good on the menu?
15. I'm not too strong on fish.

14

1. How would you like your steak?
2. What kind of sauce would you like?
3. Would you care to have for your dessert?
4. Thank you for your order.
5. Can I substitute a salad for this soup?
6. What happened to my order?
7. I want my steak well-done.
8. Would you mind waiting about ten minutes?
9. I'll be right back to take your orders.
10. Have you ever tried Korean dishes before?
11. What kind of salad dressing would you like?
12. What kind of sea food can you recommend?
13. Who is going to pay for all this , sir?
14. Shall I make out separate bills, sir?
15. Shall I take them back, sir?

15

1. Propose a toast.
2. This is on me.
3. It's so good of you to come.
4. What can I get you?
5. What would you like?
6. How would you like your martini?
7. What would you like for your side dish?
8. How much do I owe you?
9. Please show me the wine list.
10. I'd like something non-alcoholic.
11. We are not allowed to serve tea here.
12. Bring me something that's not too strong.
13. We serve beers on draft in bottles.
14. You must order a side dish if you sit at the table.
15. May I have your Key card, please?

16

1. How about trying Scotch on the rocks?
2. Shall I charge this to your room?
3. May I have your Key cards please?
4. That'll be ten thousand won.
5. Can I order other drinks that way?
6. I wish to propose a toast to Mr. Kim.
7. Would you like ice and lemon in that?
8. What would you like to drink?
9. What kind of side would you like?
10. What kind of whisky do you have?
11. A double martini, and make it strong. Without ice.
12. Can you charge what I've just had to my room number?
13. What will you have?
14. Can I have the bill, please?
15. Which one would you prefer?

17

1. Would you like separate checks?
2. Do we pay you or the cashier?
3. We are ready to leave now.
4. I'll have it ready in a moment.
5. This is our first time here.
6. Do you need cream and sugar?
7. Give me an orange juice.
8. I hope you enjoyed your meal.
9. How would you like to pay, sir?
10. Do you accept foreign currency?
11. What kind have you got?
12. This is your change.
13. I hope we serve you again.
14. We are preparing your meal now.
15. May I take your meal tray, sir?

18

1. May I help you with your baggage?
2. I'm a tour escort of Korean package tour.
3. How many people in your party?
4. How many baggage do you have, sir?
5. I want to check in now.
6. I'll show you.
7. Here we are.
8. Here is the name list of the guests.
9. See you later.
10. Enjoy your stay.
11. Do you have any reservation letter?
12. How are you going to pay, sir?
13. Here are you Keys and coupons for your breakfast.
14. Your baggage will be delivered by bellman soon.
15. May I put your baggage over there?

19

1. Could you help me to find the bank near by?
2. You can't miss it on your right.
3. How can I get to city hall?
4. This is my first visit here.
5. How long does it take walking from here?
6. It takes about fifteen minutes.
7. The street signs are located at the intersection areas.
8. I'd like a gift for my wife.
9. Can you recommend something?
10. Can you tell me the way to the disco, please?
11. What can I do for you?
12. I'd like to cash my traveler's checks.
13. How would you like it?
14. I'd like to change Korean won into dollars, please.
15. Please fill out this form.

20

1. How much is this dinner set?
2. What kind of design do you have?
3. What about the prices?
4. The price is too high for me.
5. The price is also moderate.
6. Will you buy it?
7. Can you fix it by tomorrow?
8. Don't worry about that.
9. What color would you like to buy, ma'am?
10. How about this one?
11. It will go very well with you, I think.
12. I'm looking for a robot.
13. I'm just looking around.
14. Just relax and let you look around.
15. Thank you for your kindness.

21

1. I'd like to see a suit.
2. Won't you try on this?
3. Do you want a tailor-made suit?
4. What kind of cloth is it made of?
5. What color are you interested in?
6. What size do you wear?
7. These are a little tight.
8. It seems to fit you well, sir.
9. Please wrap these for me.
10. They're a little expensive.
11. It's a good buy at that price.
12. That is not for sale.
13. I'm sure you will be happy with this pants.
14. This is a new fashion.
15. Will you accept a credit card?

22

1. What are you shopping for?
2. I want to see that one in the window.
3. That is perfect for you.
4. What material are those?
5. Would you like to buy any duty-free items, ma'am?
6. What kinds of cigarettes do you sell?
7. May I take your order for any duty-free items, sir?
8. How much is it in won?
9. I'm sorry to have kept you waiting, sir.
10. What sort of watch do you want?
11. How much do you expect it to be?
12. It seems too large for a girl.
13. Can't you take off three thousand won?
14. We are not allowed to make reductions in price.
15. We only sell at fixed price.

23

1. I would like to rent a car.
2. What kind of car do you want, sir?
3. May I see your brochure?
4. What's the abbreviation for SM?
5. I'll take this one.
6. May I see your driving license?
7. Do you have any identification cards besides this?
8. What's the rental charge?
9. For how long do you want to rent a car?
10. The average daily rate is fifty dollars for 24 hours, plus ten cents per mile, sir.
11. What items are included in the rental charge?
12. It includes gas, oil and insur ance.
13. Where do you want to leave the car?
14. Can I leave it at any of Hart office?
15. You can leave it at any of our office.

24

1. Do I have to visit the tour information center?
2. What's the destination of our tour today?
3. We are going to a famous Farm House.
4. May I ask you of the schedule?
5. What will we experience after dinner?
6. You'll have a chance to take a picture with the sheep.
7. You'll be devided into three groups.
8. We'll be too busy to follow the schedule.
9. I'll give you a morning call at five.
10. What about the schedule in the afternoon?
11. We will have optional tours until tomorrow evening.
12. I'll recommand two option courses for you.
13. Do we have to pay for that?
14. It will cost you about US $100.
15. What's the purpose of your visit?

25

1. May I help you?
2. I'd like to make a collect call to Seoul.
3. May I have your name, please.
4. Hold on a second, sir.
5. Could you occept the charges?
6. If you want, you may use the Direct International Call System.
7. How can I do that, operator?
8. Well, first dil 011 for international call.
9. It's very convenient and simple.
10. I'll try it right now.
11. Have a sound sleep, sir.
12. I'd like to talk with Mr. Park.
13. I'll connect you with the room, 1234.
14. I'll try to call him again later.
15. The line is busy now.

26

1. May I help you?
2. Could I speak to professor kim, please?
3. May I ask who's calling, please?
4. Hold on, please.
5. I'll see if he is in.
6. He's on the other line at the moment.
7. I'll call back later.
8. Would you tell me when he'll be back?
9. Would you give me your name and phone number?
10. I'd like to make an appointment with professor Kim, please.
11. I'll connect you with Mr. Kim.
12. I've got a free day today.
13. What kind of entertainment does this town offer?
14. We've got an information brochure here, sir.
15. We can get tickets for you, sir, if you want.

27

1. I'd like to reconfirm the reservations.
2. You've reserved on the flight, NW 021.
3. I've reserved 20 people on the same flight.
4. Let me check it.
5. I'll reconfirm it as your request.
6. Please come to the airport at least two hours before flight time, sir.
7. Have a nice trip.
8. Thank you for your waiting, sir.
9. Do you know your reservation number?
10. There must have been some mistake.
11. It's our mistake, sir.
12. Do you want to fly by first class or economy class?
13. Do you have the flight departing at that time?
14. What time would you like to make it?
15. I'd like to reserve a seat for a flight to New York on July 21.

28

1. When are you leaving?
2. Any flight on Saturday ofternoon?
3. Yes, we have at 5 p.m.
4. I will take it.
5. Your reservation is cancelled.
6. I'd like to confirm my reservation.
7. May I have your air-ticket and travel document?
8. Would you like economy class or first class?
9. Would you like a window seat or an isle seat, sir?
10. Would you put your baggage on the scale, sir?
11. Would you like a round trip ticket?
12. What is the flight schedule for tomorrow?
13. What time do I have to be at the airport for that flight?
14. I'd like to change my flight schedule.
15. I'll change it for you.

29

1. I want to check-in, please.
2. May I see your ticket and passport, please.
3. Are you going to Los Angeles on Flight 021?
4. Do you have any baggage to check?
5. I'll carry this briefcase myself.
6. Please empty your pockets and go through again, sir.
7. Is this where I check in for Flight 021?
8. May I see your boarding pass?
9. Please the aisle to the right.
10. Your seat is in the back of the cabin, on your right.
11. May I help you find your seat?
12. This way, please.
13. May I help you with your belongings, sir?
14. If you need anything during the flight, please let us know.
15. Do you have any empty seats together.

30

1. My wife is sitting over there, and we want to sit together.
2. It is a smoking zone.
3. We have to keep the aisle open.
4. Where can I put my bag?
5. Would you mind putting out your ciger, please?
6. Would you care for something to drink?
7. Would you mind fastening the seat belt?
8. If you need any help, just push this call button.
9. Please put your bag under the seat in front of you.
10. Would you like a newspaper or a magazine, sir?
11. Where is my seat located?
12. May I smoke now?
13. This is my first travel by air.
14. May I have your attention, please?
15. May I have some pills for it?

❖ Unit 2 ❖

Section Ⅰ

1. Do you mind if I stay for a while?

(A) Suit yourself.

(B) I found it this afternoon.

(C) I must have left it somewhere.

✐ 잠시 머물러도 괜찮을까요?

✐ 좋으실대로 하세요

2. Did you hear anything especially interesting?

(A) I didn't feel much surprise.

(B) Just the usual thing.

(C) You must have dropped it.

✐ 특별히 재미있는 소식있어요?

✐ 그냥 평범한 것밖에 없어요.

3. May I help you with your breakfast?

(A) Good morning

(B) I'm not hungry,

(C) I don't want to.

✐ 아침식사 차려드릴까요?

✐ 배 안고파요

4. When was this picture taken?

(A) Everyone always has.

(B) Who told you?

(C) I can't remember.

✐ 이 사진 언제 찍었어요?

✐ 기억이 안나요

5. You'll give me the details when everything is set?

(A) I'm only trying to help.

(B) Sure. Probably in a couple of weeks.

(C) I just wanted to make sure you'd join us.

✐ 모든 것이 준비되면 자세히 알려주시겠어요?

✐ 물론이죠. 아마 2주 후면 되겠습니다.

6. **Would you like to go on a helicopter ride?**

(A) I'd like that.

(B) There are planes out there.

(C) He didn't want to.

✐ 헬리콥터를 타고 가시겠습니까?

✐ 저도 그러고 싶습니다.

7. **Is this where the accident happened?**

(A) It's hard to remember.

(B) I fell off my horse.

(C) I don't know when he comes.

✐ 이곳이 바로 사건이 난 곳입니까?

✐ 기억하기가 어렵다.

8. **Did I send for you?**

(A) I'm going away.

(B) I'm here of my own free will.

(C) You keep in touch.

✐ 내가 너를 부르러 보냈니?

✐ 저는 자진해서 여기 왔습니다.

9. What's all this about resigning?

(A) A likely story

(B) I'm leaving the country.

(C) I'll be in touch.

✎ 도대체 왜 사직했습니까?

✎ 이 나라를 떠납니다.

10. Do you think he might be glad of some support from his friends?

(A) Why don't you give it a try?

(B) They are old friends, I believe.

(C) I'm afraid he is.

✎ 그의 친구들이 지지하면 그가 기뻐할까요?

✎ 한번 시도해 보시죠.

11. I hope I'm not intruding.

(A) I'm going on there now.

(B) I'll be off now.

(C) It was good of you to come.

✎ 방해가 안 되었으면 합니다.

✎ 당신이 와서 기뻤습니다.

12. Could I see your medical records?

(A) Don't walk too far.

(B) Here you are.

(C) I've never thought that before.

✐ 당신의 진료기록을 볼 수 있겠습니까?

✐ 여기 있습니다.

13. Do you want to talk to me about anything?

(A) I've been very busy.

(B) I miss them too.

(C) No, nothing.

✐ 나에게 뭔가 얘기하고 싶니?

✐ 아뇨, 아무 것도.

14. I expect you're going down to the ranch this weekend, aren't you?

(A) I'm catching the 9:00 o'clock plane tomorrow morning.

(B) I'm sure it's fine.

(C) I've been expecting you.

✐ 이번 주말에 농장에 내려가니?

✐ 내일 아침 9시 비행기를 타고 갈 겁니다.

15. How about making a date for the first Wednesday in October?

(A) Let me check my calendar.

(B) Take care of yourself.

(C) Yes, that was it.

✐ 10월 첫째 수요일에 데이트 하는 게 어때?

✐ 달력 좀 확인할게.

16. Where did you go on vacation?

(A) Last Saturday

(B) It was fantastic.

(C) To a resort

✐ 휴가 어디로 갔었니?

✐ 유원지로

17. What qualifications does he have for the job?

(A) She's got a B.A.

(B) He's finished college.

(C) They have two years' experience.

✐ 그 일을 하는데 그는 어떤 자격이 있죠?

✐ 대학을 졸업했다.

18. What time is the meeting going to be finished?

(A) It'll be over after one.

(B) It's time for lunch.

(C) We're meeting tomorrow.

✐ 그 모임은 몇시에 끝나죠?

✐ 1시 이후에 끝난다.

19. When did the doctor say you could go back to work?

(A) He said tomorrow would be okay.

(B) He said he's going tomorrow.

(C) He said I had a bad cold.

✐ 네가 언제 직장에 복귀할 수 있다고 의사 선생님이 말했어?

✐ 내일이 좋겠다고 말씀하셨어.

20. Could you please fill out this form for me?

(A) Sure. Here's my seat.

(B) Okay. I'm combing my hair.

(C) Fine. I need to use your pen.

✐ 내 대신 이 서식에 기입해 주시겠어요?

✐ 좋아요, 당신 펜을 사용하겠습니다.

21. How does my suit look?

(A) It fits you very well.

(B) There's a spot on your shirt.

(C) Your shoes look great.

✐ 내 양복 어때?

✐ 당신에게 아주 잘 맞아요.

22. Can I park the car on this street?

(A) I think it's illegal.

(B) We don't need any vases.

(C) No. It's too far from here.

✐ 이 거리에 주차시킬 수 있어요?

✐ 그건 불법인 것 같아요.

23. Do you have the time?

(A) It's a quarter of three.

(B) I was very busy.

(C) I'll see you soon.

✐ 몇 시입니까?

✐ 3시 15분전입니다.

24. What did you think about the new Kevin Costner movie?

(A) I enjoyed it.

(B) It's very nice.

(C) I will enjoy it.

✐ 케빈 코스트너의 새 영화 어땠어?

✐ 아주 재미있게 봤어요.

25. Have you looked over our accounting records?

(A) Thanks. I'm looking for it.

(B) Yes, I've seen him before.

(C) Yes, I've checked them already.

✐ 우리 회계기록 검토하셨어요?

✐ 예, 벌써 확인 다 했습니다.

26. Does this man repair shoes here?

(A) He fixes soles and heels.

(B) This one probably mends trousers.

(C) He knows how to repair zippers.

✐ 이분이 여기서 구두 수선하세요?

✐ 그는 구두창과 뒷굽을 수리합니다.

27. Will you be going away for the weekend?

(A) No, I don't have any time off.

(B) I've already been to the mountains.

(C) I plan to be back on time.

✐ 주말에 어디 멀리 가실겁니까?

✐ 아뇨, 짬낼 시간이 없어요.

28. Do you know if this bus goes to 34th Street?

(A) Yeah, we're both 34.

(B) Yes, this is bus number four.

(C) Yeah, it runs along that street.

✐ 이 버스가 34번가로 가는지, 안 가는지 아세요?

✐ 예, 그 거리를 따라 운행합니다.

29. Are you new to the company?

(A) No. Mr. Jones knows me.

(B) No. I know many companies.

(C) No. I started last month.

✐ 그 회사에 처음이세요?

✐ 아뇨, 지난달부터 다녔어요.

30. When can you have this report finished?

(A) I've worked on his report already.

(B) We're now completing the finishing touches.

(C) We've finished their report.

✐ 이 보고서 언제 끝낼 수 있어요?

✐ 우리는 지금 마무리 손질을 끝내고 있어요.

Section II

1. What kind of film do you use in your camera?

(A) I like to take action pictures.

(B) I generally use color exposure.

(C) I have an instant camera.

✐ 사진기에 어떤 필름을 쓰니?

✐ 일반적으로 컬러필름을 사용해.

2. Where did Martha call at 4:30 p.m.?

(A) Martha called from a phone booth.

(B) She was in her office.

(C) She called home around 4:30.

✐ Martha가 오후 4시 30분에 어디에 전화했니?

✐ 약 4시 30분 쯤 집에 전화했다.

3. Who went with you to the movies last night?

(A) We saw a great movie.

(B) My friend couldn't go with me.

(C) I went by myself to see the movie.

✐ 어젯밤 영화구경 누구하고 갔어?

✐ 혼자서 보러 갔어.

4. Will you be attending the banquet on the fifteenth?

(A) Thanks, but I'm on a diet.

(B) Thanks, but I've already been invited.

(C) Certainly, I'll be there.

✐ 15일날 그 잔치에 참석하실 겁니까?

✐ 물론, 거기 갈 겁니다.

5. Hi Emma, how are you?

(A) Oh, I'm going to the store.

(B) So-so. How about you?

(C) Bye Bill. Nice talking to you.

✐ 안녕, 에마. 어떻게 지내?

✐ 그저 그래, 너는 어때?

6. Did you attend the seminar last month in Washington?

(A) I wanted to, but I couldn't.

(B) I was there once five years ago.

(C) Yes, I'd like to very much.

✐ 지난달 워싱턴에서 있었던 세미나에 참석했었니?

✐ 가고 싶었지만, 갈 수가 없었어.

7. What are your new work hours?

(A) I'll earn eight dollars an hour.

(B) It's from 9 to 4.

(C) They're 10 to 5.

✐ 새로 바뀐 근무시간은 언제야?

✐ 10시부터 5시까지야.

8. Does your job pay well?

(A) Yes, I get an adequate amount.

(B) yes, they paid me.

(C) yes, it will.

✐ 당신의 직장은 보수가 좋습니까?

✐ 네, 충분한 금액을 받고 있어요.

9. Do you know today's date?

(A) It's Saturday.

(B) Our date's for today.

(C) It's the twelfth.

✐ 오늘이 몇 일인지 아니?

✐ 12일입니다.

10. Have you seen my wallet?

(A) I think you bought it.

(B) No, I don't have it.

(C) Yeah, it looks great.

✐ 내 지갑 본 적있니?

✐ 예, 그것 멋져 보여요.

11. Did you take my umbrella?

(A) No, that's not mine.

(B) No, it isn't raining.

(C) No, it wasn't necessary.

✐ 내 우산 가져갔니?

✐ 아뇨, 우산 필요없었어요.

12. What would you like to order for lunch?

(A) We're on a diet.

(B) Just soup and salad.

(C) I don't like anything.

✐ 점심으로 뭘 주문하시겠습니까?

✐ 스프와 샐러드만.

13. Do you want to go to a movie?

(A) I think it won an Academy Award.

(B) The theater doesn't look very crowded.

(C) I don't think I can afford it.

✐ 영화보러 갈래?

✐ 그럴 여유가 없을 것 같아요.

14. May I buy you some ice cream?

(A) Thanks. I like strawberry.

(B) Thanks, but I don't like them.

(C) No thanks. I have many of them.

✐ 아이스크림 좀 사 드릴까요?

✐ 고마워요. 난 딸기 아이스크림이 좋아요.

15. Hello. May I speak to Harry, please?

(A) No, thank you.

(B) Just a minute.

(C) I'm sorry we haven't any here.

✐ 여보세요, 해리씨 좀 바꿔주세요.

✐ 잠깐만 기다리세요.

16. When is the bus arriving?

(A) In ten minutes

(B) Ten times a day

(C) Ten minutes ago

✐ 버스는 언제 도착하나요?

✐ 10분 후에

17. How about joining me for dinner tonight?

(A) I don't want it.

(B) I'd like that.

(C) I'd like to eat that.

✐ 오늘 밤 나하고 함께 저녁하는 게 어때?

✐ 나도 그러고 싶습니다.

18. Did you finish the project?

(A) I'm going on vacation next week.

(B) I'm finishing work at five o'clock.

(C) Yes, and it's ready to be examined.

✐ 그 프로젝트 끝났어?

✐ 예, 이제 검토될 준비가 됐습니다.

19. How much are we in debt?

(A) In three hours

(B) About 30,000 dollars

(C) In a million years

✐ 우리가 빚진 게 얼마야?

✐ 약 3만 달러입니다.

20. Is the new account executive nice?

(A) No, she is.

(B) No, I don't want to.

(C) No, I don't think so.

✐ 새로 온 회계과 이사 좋아요?

✐ 아니, 그런 것 같지 않아요.

21. Is the copy machine broken?

(A) Yes, it is.

(B) No, I'm not.

(C) Yes, it's fixed.

✐ 복사기 고장 났어?

✐ 예, 그래요.

22. When do you think we'll be taking off?

(A) Your hat and coat, please.

(B) In about twenty minutes

(C) An hour ago

✐ 우리가 언제 이륙할 거라고 생각하세요?

✐ 약 20분 후에

23. Have you seen the sales report for this quarter?

(A) Yes, and it doesn't look good.

(B) No, I don't have any change.

(C) No, it isn't sold yet.

✐ 이번 분기 영업보고서 봤어요?

✐ 예, 그것은 별로 좋지 않은 것 같아요.

24. Aren't we supposed to have a meeting at three o'clock?

(A) For about an hour

(B) No, it's been put off until tomorrow.

(C) No, I posted it already.

✐ 우리 3시에 모임을 하기로 되어 있지 않나요?

✐ 네, 그러나 내일로 연기되었어요.

25. Will we be met at the airport by someone from your firm?

(A) Yes, he'll take you there.

(B) He arrives at ten o'clock.

(C) No, I'm afraid you'll have to take a taxi.

✐ 당신의 우리를 마중하러 회사사람이 공항으로 나올겁니까?

✐ 아뇨, 택시를 타셔야만 될 것 같은데요.

26. Is that position still open in the personnel office?

(A) I think it was filled last week.

(B) Yes, could you close it please?

(C) He's standing there next to the desk.

✐ 인사과의 그 자리는 아직 공석인가요?

✐ 그 자리는 지난주에 찬 것 같습니다.

27. Is it true you put in for a transfer to London?

(A) Yes, but I didn't like it there.

(B) Yes, but only if I get a promotion as well.

(C) Yes, I hope he gets it.

✐ 런던에 전근 가는데 당신이 응시했다는 게 사실입니까?

✐ 예, 그러나, 그것 또한 진급을 해야만 가능합니다.

28. Will you be coming for tea on Tuesday?

(A) Sorry, I'm tied up all day.

(B) Thanks, I love it.

(C) No, I don't like those.

✐ 화요일 날 차 한 잔 하러 오시겠습니까?

✐ 미안합니다. 하루 종일 바빠서요.

29. Will you be around tomorrow after work?

(A) No, I had a new job.

(B) No, I have to go straight home.

(C) No, I'll work until then.

✐ 내일 퇴근 후에 부근에 계실건가요?

✐ 아뇨, 집에 곧장 가야 합니다.

30. Have you spent much time working on this report?

(A) Sorry, but I'm very busy today.

(B) About two hours, and it's still not finished.

(C) No, it was quite inexpensive.

✐ 이 보고서 작성하는데 시간이 많이 들었어요?

✐ 약 2시간 정도. 그런데도 아직 안 끝났어요.

Section Ⅲ

1. Do you regret not accepting that transfer?

(A) Not really. I'm happy here.

(B) No, I can't accept it at this time.

(C) Yes, I'd like that very much.

✐ 부서이동을 받아들이지 않은 것을 후회합니까?

✐ 저는 정말 후회하지 않아요. 저는 여기서 행복해요.

2. How do you want to pay this bill?

(A) I'd like to use my credit card.

(B) Yes, I paid it last week.

(C) At the bank on the corner

✐ 당신은 이 계산서를 어떻게 지불하기를 원하세요?

✐ 저는 신용카드를 사용하고 싶습니다.

3. Why is he leaving the meeting so soon?

(A) Yes, that's a good idea.

(B) He has another appointment.

(C) Yes, at about three o'clock p.m.

✐ 왜 그는 그 모임에서 그렇게 빨리 떠나지요?

✐ 그는 다른 약속이 있습니다.

4. Haven't you been waiting here a long time?

(A) Yes, but I need to see the president today.

(B) Only until this afternoon.

(C) Yes, but I got bored, so I left.

✐ 당신은 오랫동안 여기서 기다려 오지 않았나요?

✐ 아닙니다. 저는 오늘 사장을 만나야겠습니다.

5. Don't you agree that Tom has all the necessary experience for this position?

(A) Yes, I think he will.

(B) Yes, he found them in the drawer.

(C) Yes, but not the education.

✐ 당신은 Tom이 이 직책을 위한 모든 필요한 경험을 가지고 있다는 것에 동의하지 않습니까?

✐ 아니요, 저는 동의합니다. 그러나 Tom이 이 직책을 위한 교육을 받은 것에 대해서는 동의하지 않습니다.

6. Would you like us to reserve a room for you at the hotel?

(A) No, thanks. I did it already.

(B) Yes, you have. But I don't like it.

(C) Yes, it's a very nice room.

✐ 당신은 우리가 당신을 위해 호텔에 방 하나를 예약하기를 원합니까?

✐ 감사합니다만, 저는 이미 예약을 했어요.

7. Can I depend on you to be on time for work?

(A) I give you my word.

(B) I've given it a lot of thought.

(C) Yes. I arrived at four o'clock.

✐ 당신이 직장에 정각에 온다는 것을 제가 믿을 수 있을까요?

✐ 약속합니다.

8. Do you approve of the way I organized these files?

(A) Actually, it could have been done better.

(B) Yes, I suppose you're right.

(C) I agree. It definitely needs to be done.

✐ 제가 이 서류들을 정리한 방식에 동의합니까?

✐ 사실, 더 잘 정리될 수도 있었을 텐데요.

9. Do you think we should hire a new secretary to replace Julia?

(A) Yes, she's doing quite well.

(B) I don't think that we need to at this time.

(C) That was a good idea.

✐ 우리가 Julia를 대신할 새로운 비서를 고용해야 한다고 당신은 생각합니까?

✐ 우리는 이번에 새로운 비서를 고용할 필요가 있다고 생각하지는 않는다.

10. This new computer works well, but wouldn't you agree that it was a bit too expensive for our budget?

(A) You have a point, there.

(B) Yes, I know it does.

(C) No, it won't be.

✐ 이 새로운 컴퓨터는 기능이 좋습니다. 그러나 그것은 우리 예산 내에서 다소 값이 비싼 것이었다는 데에 당신은 동의하지 않습니까?

✐ 당신 말에 일리가 있습니다.

11. Why hasn't Carol come into the office yet today?

(A) She's thinking about it.

(B) She's sick today.

(C) Yes, she will later.

✐ 왜 Carol은 오늘 사무실에 아직 오지 않았습니까?

✐ 오늘 그 여자는 몸이 아프기 때문입니다.

12. Are you a college graduate or not?

(A) My father is a doctor.

(B) I'm still in high school.

(C) Next week is exam week.

✐ 당신은 대학졸업생입니까? 대학졸업생이 아닙니까?

✐ 저는 아직 고등학교에 다닙니다.

13. What do you think of the new general manager?

(A) Yes, I think he will.

(B) I don't know. I haven't met him yet.

(C) I believe he did.

✐ 당신은 그 새로운 총지배인에 대해 어떻게 생각합니까?

✐ 저는 알지 못합니다. 저는 그를 아직 만나 본적이 없습니다.

14. Should I have prepared this report differently?

(A) No, I wouldn't if I were you.

(B) Yes, you really should.

(C) No, it seems all right to me.

✐ 제가 다르게 이 보고서를 준비했어야만 했습니까?

✐ 아니요, 저에게는 그것이 괜찮아 보이는데요.

15. How do you like the way I introduced you to the audience?

(A) I think you did very well.

(B) Yes, it seems that you did.

(C) No, you shouldn't have done it.

✐ 당신은 제가 당신을 소개했던 방법이 마음에 드십니까?

✐ 저는 당신이 아주 잘 소개했다고 생각합니다.

16. Have you heard from Robert recently?

(A) My brother's name is Robert.

(B) I'm not going there.

(C) No, I haven't

✐ 당신은 최근에 Robert로부터 소식을 들었습니까?

✐ 아니요, 저는 듣지 못했습니다.

17. Are you sick today?

(A) I don't feel well.

(B) I went to Switzerland yesterday.

(C) I want to go home now.

✐ 당신은 오늘 아픈가요?

✐ 저는 몸이 좋지 않아요.

18. Are you his mother?

(A) I'll be there soon.

(B) He's not married.

(C) No, he's my nephew.

✐ 당신이 그의 어머니입니까?

✐ 아니요, 그는 나의 조카입니다.

19. Do you take anything in your coffee?

(A) Just black, please.

(B) I've had lunch.

(C) I'm very hungry.

✐ 당신은 커피에 어떤 것을 타서 마십니까?

✐ 그냥 블랙커피주세요.

20. Was the plane on schedule?

(A) No, we were delayed in Pittsburgh.

(B) I flew first class.

(C) We had lunch on the plane.

✐ 비행기는 예정대로 도착했습니까?

✐ 아니요, 우리는 Pittsburgh에서 지체되었어요.

21. What did she say about me?

(A) She was an acrobat.

(B) Nothing bad.

(C) I'm still hungry.

✐ 그 여자는 나에 관해 무엇을 말했습니까?

✐ 그 여자는 당신에 관해서 나쁜 것을 말하지 않았습니다.

22. Have the brochures been sent out?

(A) I'll send out for coffee.

(B) They went out in this morning's mail.

(C) I don't know who they sent.

✐ 그 팜플렛을 보냈습니까?

✐ 그것들은 아침 우편으로 나갔습니다.

23. How are the sales projections for next year?

(A) They look pretty promising.

(B) The project was completed.

(C) Last year wasn't too bad.

✐ 내년의 판매계획들은 어떻습니까?

✐ 그들은 아주 전망이 좋아 보입니다.

24. Do you want coffee or tea?

(A) I want to tear up the copy.

(B) Not now. Maybe later thanks.

(C) I've been coughing all day.

✐ 당신은 커피를 원합니까? 또는 차를 원합니까?

✐ 지금은 생각이 없고, 잠시 후에 마시겠습니다. 감사합니다.

25. Where's the letterhead stationery kept?

(A) At the corner drugstore

(B) After the meeting

(C) In the bottom drawer

✐ 주소가 인쇄된 편지지가 어디에 보관되어 있습니까?

✐ 하단부 서랍에 있습니다.

26. Can I have a copy of the sales figures for June?

(A) I put one on your desk.

(B) What do you like in your coffee?

(C) He can't figure it out.

✐ 제가 6월 판매액의 복사본 하나를 가져도 될까요?

✐ 제가 당신 책상 위에 하나를 갖다 놓았습니다.

27. Why doesn't he change jobs?

(A) He doesn't have any change.

(B) He's got too much seniority to quit now.

(C) Because it's raining.

✐ 왜 그는 직업을 바꾸지 않습니까?

✐ 그는 너무나 연장자이므로 지금 포기할 수가 없다.

28. May I have five thirty-cent stamps, please?

(A) Okay. That'll be $1.50.

(B) You can take them home.

(C) Thank you for your advice.

✐ 30센트짜리 우표 5장 주세요.

✐ 알겠습니다. 값은 1달러 50센트입니다.

29. How about giving me a hand typing these reports?

(A) Sure, here you are.

(B) I'd like to, but I don't know how to type.

(C) You can do them any way you like.

✐ 이 보고서를 타자로 쳐주시겠어요?

✐ 제가 돕고 싶습니다만, 타자치는 방법을 모릅니다.

30. Did she tell you about her plans?

(A) I don't have any more for you.

(B) Yes. She has been explaining them all morning.

(C) The plans will be ready for publication shortly.

✐ 그 여자는 자신의 계획들에 대해 당신에게 말했습니까?

✐ 예, 그 여자는 아침 내내 그 계획들을 설명했습니다.

❖ Unit 3 ❖

Section I

1. *A : How long will it take for the package to arrive?*

   B : Four business days.

   A : Then if I mail it Thursday, it should get there in time.

   A : 이 소포 도착하는데 얼마나 걸리죠?

   B : 주말 빼고 4일 걸립니다.

   A : 그럼 목요일에 부치면 제때 거기 도달하겠네요.

When will the package arrive?

(A) On Monday

(B) On Friday

(C) On Wednesday

(D) On Thursday

2. *A : I attended a really interesting conference last weekend on how to expand our international market.*

   B : Really? Was that the one held downtown?

   A : No, that one was about how to boost domestic sales. The one I went to was held out-of-town.

A : 지난 주말에 아주 재미있는 회의에 참석했는데, 우리 국제시장을 어떻게 확장하느냐에 관한 것이었어.

B : 정말? 그것 시내에서 개최된 회의였지?

A : 아니, 네가 말하는 것은 국내 영업신장에 관한 것이었고, 내가 갔던 것은 시외에서 했어.

What happened over the weekend?

(A) The man went to a conference downtown.

(B) The man went to an international market.

(C) A conference about international markets was held downtown.

(D) There was an interesting conference held out-of-town.

3. *A : Do you have any vcancy?*

B : Yes, we will have one room, but it's only a single, and it's not available until noon.

A : That'll do. Here's our deposit. We'll be back.

A : 빈 방 있습니까?

B : 예, 방이 1개 나올텐데요, 그것도 싱글룸 1개 밖에는 안되고, 12시나 지나야 가능합니다.

A : 그것도 좋습니다. 계약금 여기 있습니다. 나중에 오겠습니다.

Where are they?

(A) At a sports complex with tennis courts

(B) At a hotel

(C) At an apartment complex

(D) At a travel agency

4. *A : The company will reimburse you for mileage.*

B : What about my travel expenditures for food and lodging?

A : Those must come out of your own pocket this time.

A : 회사가 마일당 여비를 지급할 겁니다.

B : 숙식비 지출은 어떡하고?

A : 그건 이번에는 당신 돈으로 써야만 합니다.

What will the company pay for?

(A) Only gas

(B) All travel expenditures

(C) Food and lodging only

(D) Food, lodging, and mileage

5. *A : Could I borrow the most recent issue of the journal you subscribe to?*

B : Unfortunately, it expired six months ago.

A : Do you know anyone else who subscribes to it?

A : 당신이 구독하는 잡지의 최근호를 빌릴 수 있어?

B : 안됐지만, 6개월 전에 구독이 만료되었어.

A : 너 말고 그것 구독하는 사람 아니?

What is said about subscribing to the journal?

(A) The man no longer receives the subscription.

(B) The man began subscribing six months ago.

(C) No one else subscribes to the journal.

(D) Everyone else subscribes to the journal.

6. *A : Do I have to remind you about the dress code again?*

B : But I thought today was a more-relaxed schedule.

A : Yes, it is. But the dress code still stands.

A : 옷 차림새에 대해 당신에게 다시 알려줘야 할까?

B : 저는 오늘 일정이 좀 완화된 날이라고 생각했어요.

A : 그렇긴 하지만, 옷 차림새에 관한 규약은 여전히 유효해.

Why is the boss angry?

(A) Because the employee sat down at the wrong time.

(B) Because the employee did not wear a dress.

(C) Because the employee did not have the appropriate attire.

(D) Because the employee was too relaxed about the schedule.

7. *A : Are you planning a trip to Japan?*

B : Yes, I am. I will visit Kyoto for sure.

A : Sounds good.

A : 일본으로 여행갈 계획이세요?

B : 예, 꼭 쿄토를 방문할 겁니다.

A : 좋은 생각입니다.

What are the men talking about?

(A) About their trip to Japan last year

(B) About planning a meeting

(C) About Japanese cars

(D) About a trip to Japan

8. *A : Did I tell you I got a letter from Bill yesterday?*

B : No, you didn't. How's he doing?

A : Pretty good. He wrote he's going to study in France this summer.

A : 어제 빌한테 편지 받았다고 내가 얘기했나?

B : 아니. 그 사람 어떻게 지내?

A : 아주 좋대. 이번 여름에 프랑스에서 공부할거라고 썼어.

What is true about Bill?

(A) He received a letter.

(B) He is French.

(C) He will study abroad.

(D) He spent his summer in France.

9. *A : Who should I see about the position that's open?*

B : Ask for the Personnel Manager at the front desk.

A : Thank you. I hope it hasn't been filled yet.

A : 공석으로 있는 자리에 대해 알아보려면 누구를 만나야 합니까?

B : 프론트에서 인사부장을 요청하세요.

A : 고맙습니다. 아직 그 자리가 안 찼으면 좋겠는데.

Where is the first man going?

(A) To a hotel

(B) To a job interview

(C) To a pharmacy

(D) To see his boss.

10. *A : I'd like two tickets to New York, please.*

B : Here you are. The driver will collect the tickets on board.

A : Thank you. Will we be stopping for lunch?

A : 뉴욕행 표 2장 주세요.

B : 여기 있습니다. 타시면 운전사가 표를 회수할 겁니다.

A : 고맙습니다. 점심식사 때 버스가 멈추나요?

Where does this conversation take place?

(A) At a bus terminal

(B) At an airport

(C) At a train station

(D) At a taxi stand

11. *A : Could I make an appointment to see Dr. Smith?*

B : How about next Wednesday? We can fit you in then.

A : Could you make it sooner? I have a bad toothache.

A : 스미스 박사와 만날 약속을 할 수 있을까요?

B : 다음 수요일 어떠세요? 그때 약속을 해드릴 수 있는데요.

A : 더 빨리 안 될까요? 치통이 심하거는요.

When will the man see Dr. Smith?

(A) Today

(B) On Wednesday

(C) As soon as they can fit her in

(D) We don't know.

12. *A : I'd like to make a collect call to Joe Brown in Chicago.*

B : Certainly. Who is calling?

A : John Black in Denver.

A : 시카고에 있는 죠 브라운에게 수신인 지불통화를 하고 싶습니다.

B : 좋습니다. 누구시죠?

A : 덴버에 있는 존 블랙입니다.

What does the man want to do?

(A) Collect money from Joe Brown.

(B) Call Joe Brown on the telephone.

(C) Pay for the call to Joe Brown.

(D) Call John Black.

13. *A : How's the sales report coming?*

B : Good. I should be finished with it by the end of the week.

A : But the meeting's been moved up to Thursday. It needs to be finished by then.

A : 판매보고서 어떻게 돼가?

B : 잘 돼가. 이번 주말이면 끝나게 돼.

A : 하지만 회의가 목요일로 변경되었어. 그때까지 끝낼 필요가 있어.

› What does the woman want?

(A) She wants to have a meeting on Thursday.

(B) She wants the report finished before Thursday.

(C) She wants the report finished by the end of the week.

(D) She wants to finish writing the report.

14. *A : I went to Boston yesterday, but I forgot to call Bob.*

B : He wouldn't have been there anyway. He's a dentist in California now.

A : Oh? I didn't know he was in that field.

A : 어제 보스톤에 갔는데, 밥에게 전화 하는 것을 잊었어.

B : 어쨌든 그는 거기에 없었을 거야. 그는 지금 캘리포니아에서 치과의사 하거든.

A : 그래? 그가 그런 분야에 있었다는 것을 몰랐는데.

› What does the woman learn about Bob?

(A) He works outdoors in a field.

(B) He no longer lives in Boston.

(C) He forgot to call.

(D) He called her from California.

15. *A : Why are these fruits and vegetables so highly priced?*

B : There was a drought and the crops were damaged.

A : I hope it's better by summer.

A : 이 과일과 채소는 왜 이렇게 가격이 올랐어?

B : 가뭄 때문에 농작물이 피해를 입었지.

A : 여름에는 좀 나아져야 하는데.

What is the problem here?

(A) There was too much rain.

(B) The produce is very expensive.

(C) The fruits and vegetables are not of good quality.

(D) Transportation for fruits is very expensive.

16. *A : Will the car be ready by tomorrow?*

B : Sure. The damage is fairly minor.

A : Good. I have to drive to the airport to pick up my friend.

A : 내일까지 자동차 준비 되겠어?

B : 물론이죠. 파손된 것은 아주 경미해요.

A : 좋았어. 친구 데릴러 차를 공항에 몰고 가야만해.

Where does this conversation take place?

(A) In a parking lot

(B) In a mine

(C) In a car repair shop

(D) At an airport

17. *A : How's your new apartment downtown?*

B : It's more or less the same as my old one, except for the price.

A : Yes, living in the city is never a bargain.

A : 시내에 있는 네 새 아파트 어때?

B : 가격만 제외하곤, 우리 예전 아파트하고 대체로 같아.

A : 그래, 도시 생활은 결코 비용이 싸지 않아.

What does the man say about his new apartment?

(A) It costs less than his old one.

(B) It's exactly the same as his old one.

(C) It is more expensive than his old one.

(D) It is not near any bars because it is in the city.

18. *A : Have you heard about the Vice President?*

B : I can't say I have.

A : I'm not saying it's true, but there's a rumor going round that he's being transferred to Los Angeles.

A : 부사장에 대해서 뭐 들은 것 있어?

B : 못 들은 것 같은데.

A : 그게 사실이라고 말할 수는 없지만, 그가 로스앤젤레스로 전근 간다는 소문이 돌더라.

What is true about the Vice President?

(A) He may move to Los Angeles.

(B) He has been spreading a rumor.

(C) He will transfer someone to Los Angeles.

(D) We don't know.

19. *A : Would you like to take in a movie tonight?*

B : I hate to turn you down, but I have to work late.

A : That's all right. Maybe next week.

A : 오늘밤 영화 구경 가시겠어요?

B : 당신 요청을 거절하고 싶지 않지만, 저는 늦게까지 일해야 해요.

A : 괜찮아요. 그럼 다음 주로 하죠.

What did the woman do?

(A) She saw a movie.

(B) She refused an invitation.

(C) She set a date for the following week.

(D) She said she couldn't work late.

20. *A : Have you ever put one of these together before?*

B : No, but I don't think we'll have any trouble if we carry out the instructions exactly.

A : Well, we may as well get started.

A : 전에 이것들 중 하나를 조립해 본 적 있어요?

B : 아뇨, 하지만 설명서를 정확하게 따르면 별로 어려움이 없을 겁니다.

A : 자, 그러면 시작하는 게 좋겠군요.

What is important for these people to do?

(A) Carry the parts outside.

(B) Practice working together.

(C) Follow the instructions.

(D) Start the project soon.

21. *A : The reception is not good and the picture isn't clear.*

B : Why not change the TV antenna and see if that helps?

A : OK. I'll give that a try.

A : 텔레비전 수신이 안 좋고, 영상도 분명치가 않아요.

B : TV 안테나를 바꿔보고 그것이 도움이 되는지 알아봐.

A : 알았어. 그렇게 한 번 해 보자.

What does the man advise the woman to do?

(A) Get a new TV set.

(B) Try a new antenna.

(C) Not to change the TV set.

(D) Change the channel on the TV set.

22. *A : Do you have much experience in sales?*

B : Only selling newspapers when I was in high school.

A : I'm afraid we're looking for someone with both sales and overseas experience.

A : 판매에 경험 많아요?

B : 고등학교 다닐 때 신문판매밖에 안 해 봤어요.

A : 판매와 해외경험까지 있는 사람을 찾고 있는데요.

Where does this conversation probably take place?

(A) On a sailboat

(B) In a department store

(C) In a personnel office

(D) In a book store

23. *A : Joe seems to have lost some weight recently.*

B : Yes, he's been training hard for the football team.

A : Well, he looks better than ever.

A : 조가 최근에 살이 좀 빠진 것 같은데.

B : 예, 그는 축구팀에서 열심히 훈련을 해 왔어요.

A : 그는 전보다 훨씬 좋아 보이는데.

What has Joe been doing?

(A) Waiting for the train

(B) Playing football

(C) Looking for something he lost

(D) Exercising a lot

24. *A : I can't figure out how to fill out this form correctly.*

B : You could ask the clerk at the front desk.

A : Oh, he's busy waiting on other people.

A : 이 서식을 정확히 기입하는 법을 잘 이해할 수 없어요.

B : 프론트 직원에게 물어보시면 돼요.

A : 그는 다른 사람들 시중드느라 바빠요.

What is the man's problem?

(A) He doesn't understand the paperwork.

(B) He is waiting for the clerk.

(C) He is too busy.

(D) The clerk gave him the wrong form.

25. *A : How do you find the new dormitory?*

B : It's OK, but I'm having a hard time getting used to such a small space.

A : I found that to be the case as well.

A : 새 기숙사에 대해 어떻게 생각해?

B : 괜찮아, 하지만 좁은 공간에 익숙해 지기가 힘들어.

A : 나도 또한 그런 점이 문제가 되리라고 생각했었어.

What is the second man's problem?

(A) He can't find his case.

(B) He doesn't know where the dormitory is.

(C) His room is too small.

(D) He couldn't get the case into the dormitory.

26. *A : We really should catch the new play downtown.*

B : Yes, but let's eat beforehand.

A : If we do, they may be sold out when we arrive.

A : 우리는 꼭 시내에서 하는 새 연극을 봐야만 해.

B : 그래, 하지만 그전에 식사나 합시다.

A : 만약 그러면, 도착할 때 표가 매진될지도 몰라.

What does the woman want to do?

(A) Eat before seeing the play.

(B) See the play immediately.

(C) Catch a train going downtown.

(D) Sell their tickets to the play.

27. *A : You have your hands full. Would you like some help with those boxes?*

B : I wouldn't mind a bit.

A : It's no problem. I have some time to spare.

A : 당신 바쁘시군요. 그 상자 옮기는 것 도와드릴까요?

B : 그래 주시면 물론 좋지요.

A : 예, 문제없어요. 시간 여유가 좀 있어요.

What will the man do?

(A) Help fill up the boxes.

(B) Give his friend a dime.

(C) Take some of the boxes.

(D) Make sure his hands are clean.

28. *A : It sure is steamy today.*

B : Yes, it is. There's a lot of moisture in the air.

A : I prefer a dry climate, myself.

A : 오늘 날씨 정말로 무더워요.

B : 예, 그래요. 공기 중에 습기도 많아요.

A : 저 개인은 건조한 날씨가 더 좋아요.

What are these people saying about the weather?

(A) It is raining.

(B) They like it because it's dry.

(C) It's hot and humid.

(D) They wish it would stop raining.

29. *A : Did you join the company when Bill did in 1974?*

B : I joined it a year before he did.

A : I didn't know you have been here that long.

A : 빌이 1974년 입사했을 때 너도 회사에 들어왔니?

B : 내가 빌보다 일 년 먼저 입사했지.

A : 네가 그렇게 오래 여기 있었는지 몰랐어.

When did the second man join the company?

(A) In 1973

(B) In 1974

(C) In 1975

(D) Last year

30. *A : Have you seen my brother Dave?*

B : Yes. His height makes him stand out from the others.

A : That's true. He's easy to spot in a crowd.

A : 우리 형 데이브 봤어?

B : 그래. 그는 키가 커서 다른 사람과 구별이 잘 되지.

A : 맞아. 군중 속에서 그를 찾아내는 것은 쉬워.

What do these people say about Dave?

(A) He is standing outside.

(B) He was stopped because of the crowd.

(C) He is very tall.

(D) He has to stand in front of the others.

Comprehensive English for Hoteliers

인 쇄 / 2012년 8월 4일
발 행 / 2012년 8월 15일

저 자 / 박 만 도
발행인 / 김 창 석
발행처 / 홍익출판사

대구광역시 중구 삼덕3가 245 2
(053) 421-6700, 427-3627
등록 1987년 11월 26일 제1-107호

정가 14,000원

ISBN 978-89-7826-239-2 93740